THE **LIVING CENTRE** OF AUSTRALIA

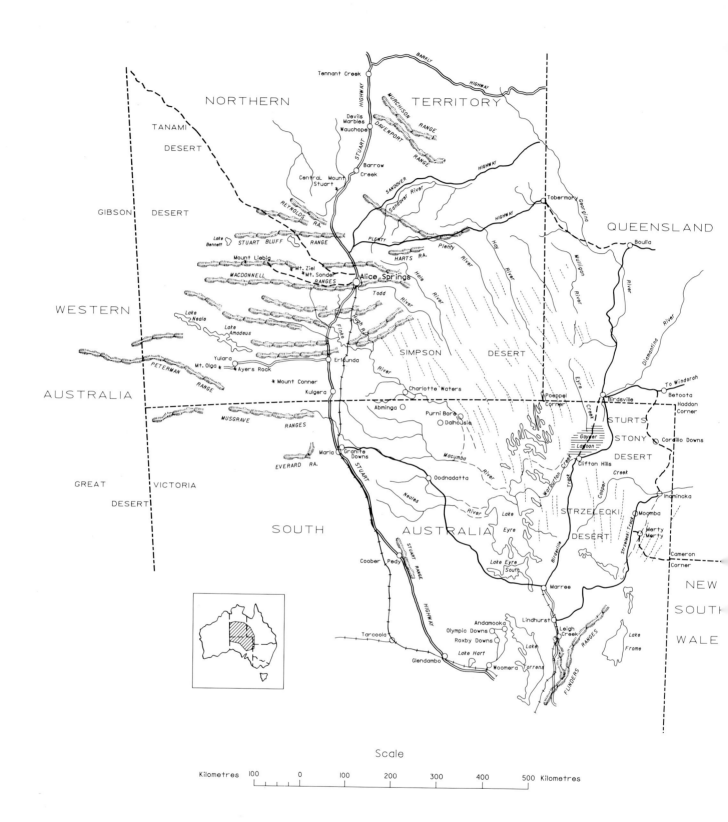

NORTHERN

TERRITORY

TANAMI

DESERT

GIBSON   DESERT

WESTERN

AUSTRALIA

Tennant Creek

Devils
Marbles
Wauchope

Barrow
Creek

Central Mount
Stuart

REYNOLDS RA.

Lake
Bennett   STUART BLUFF   RANGE

Mount Liebig
Mt. Ziel
MACDONNELL   Mt. Sonder
RANGES

Lake Neale

Lake
Amadeus

Yulara
Mt. Olga   Ayers Rock

Mount Conner

PETERMAN   RANGE

MUSGRAVE   RANGES

GREAT

VICTORIA

DESERT

EVERARD RA.

BARKLY   HIGHWAY

MURCHISON   RANGE

DAVENPORT   RANGE

STUART   HIGHWAY

SANDOVER

Sandover   River

HIGHWAY

Tobermory

Georgina

QUEENSLAND

Boulla

PLENTY

HARTS RA.   Plenty   River

Hale

Hay

River

Mulligan   River

River

Alice Springs

Todd

Finke

HIGH RA.

River

SIMPSON   DESERT

Diamantina   River

River

Erldunda

Charlotte Waters

To Windorah
Betoota

Kulgera

Abminga

Purni Bore

Dalhousia

Poeppel
Corner

Birdsville

Eyre

Creek

Haddon
Corner

SOUTH

AUSTRALIA

Marla

Granite
Downs

Macumba

River

Oodnadatta

STUART   RANGE

Neales

River

Lake

Eyre

Lake Eyre
South

Goyder
Lagoon

Clifton Hills

STURTS

STONY

DESERT

Cordillo Downs

Warburton Creek

Cooper

Creek

STRZELECKI

DESERT

Innamincka

Moomba

Birdsville

Merty
Merty

Track

Strzelecki Track

Cameron
Corner

Coober Pedy

STUART   HIGHWAY

Marree

NEW

SOUTH

WALE

Tarcoola

Andamooka

Olympic Downs

Roxby Downs

Lake Hart

Lindhurst

Lake

Leigh
Creek

RANGES

Lake
Frome

Glendambo

Woomera

Torrens

FLINDERS

Scale

Kilometres 100   0   100   200   300   400   500 Kilometres

THE
LIVING
CENTRE
OF AUSTRALIA

Alec M. Blombery

Kangaroo Press

Preface

Many books have been written on various aspects of Central Australia and no doubt, in the future, the unique character of the area will result in many more.

An illustrated book on the wildflowers of Central Australia has been under consideration by me for some time. After a visit to Alice Springs in 1983 when Ms Harvey of the Arunta Bookshop requested a book on Central Australian wildflowers on a similar pattern to my *What Wildflower is That?,* further thought was given to the subject. The scenic beauty and the impelling and unique character of the area demanded a broader approach than wildflowers only and this book is the result.

The purpose of the book is to introduce the reader to the area, emphasising its physical features and scenic beauty, showing the vegetation which has evolved, together with the dependent fauna. As an aid to recognising some of the more common plants of the area, those flowers and plants with similar appearances and characters have been grouped together, even though they belong to different plant families. For example, flowers which are tubular shaped and lipped are arranged near one another; similarly, plants which grow into trees are grouped together.

It is hoped that this book will both provide enjoyment and lead to a better understanding of the unique character of the area. For those travelling there, or planning to do so, the information provided should be of assistance, enhancing the pleasure of the visit. For the majority of readers, who may not have the opportunity to visit the area physically, it is hoped that the combination of the text and plates will provide an enjoyable mental picture of this environment.

Thanks are extended to many people for their generosity in assisting in various ways with the book, in particular to Doreen and Bill Hand of Sundowner Tours, with whom I have travelled over a number of years to various parts of Australia, and who have made many unscheduled stops to enable me to photograph and examine various subjects, at the same time offering much useful advice. Doreen has further assisted by providing transparencies of subjects which were missing from my photographic collection; other friends have also assisted with transparencies, including Heather Whiteman, John and Mark Scoble, Surrey Jacobs, Arthur Wallace and Allan Flood. Further assistance had been provided on grasses by Surrey Jacobs, who, together with the University of New England Publishing Unit, have permitted use of line drawings of grass seeds from *Grasses of New South Wales.* I wish to thank the Conservation Commission of the Northern Territory for their cooperation and permission to use a map of the Reserves of Central Australia and for other data on the area. I wish to thank Andrew Mitchell and the Herbarium of the Northern Territory, Alice Springs, for transparencies on Malvaceae.

To Bob Harris I owe a special thanks for his expertise in preparing a map of the area.

Finally, once more, to my wife Marie, my thanks for continued support and assistance in preparing a legible manuscript.

Alec M. Blombery

Reprinted in paperback 1989 and 1992
First published in 1985 by Kangaroo Press Pty Ltd
3 Whitehall Road (P.O. Box 75) Kenthurst 2156
Printed in Singapore by Kyodo Printing Co. (S'pore) Pte Ltd

ISBN 0 86417 234 6

Contents

The Physical Environment

Central Australia, as the name suggests, is the central part of the continent, with the town of Alice Springs being approximately 216 km south of the central point of Australia. For the purposes of this book, Central Australia is the area shown in Map 1. Within this vast arid region are the Lake Eyre Basin and its river systems, deserts such as the Simpson Desert, Sturt's Stony Desert, Strzelecki Desert, edges of the Victoria, Gibson and Tanami Deserts, numerous salt lakes and several mountain ranges such as the Macdonnell Ranges.

Generally access is limited to main roads and the better defined tracks, as lack of drinking water and sparse settlement on the arid, sandy and stony terrains make venturing from proper access roads extremely hazardous. Even well equipped parties with four-wheel drive vehicles, amply supplied with water and radio communication, can experience difficulties when problems occur with vehicles.

Climate

A large part of Australia is characterised by clear skies and low rainfall. This is particularly so with Central Australia, for, situated as it is in the middle of a large land mass, it lacks the prevailing moisture laden winds usually associated with proximity to the sea. This absence of moisture in the air results in a lack of cloud cover, thus providing conditions for high levels of sunshine. Records show that on an average as much as 80% of the total available sunshine throughout the year is received. The constant sunshine and low humidity bring about a high evaporation rate which is up to ten times greater than the annual rainfall. This, combined with the low rainfall, produces extremely arid conditions, hot during the day, particulary during the warmer parts of the year, but relatively cool at night. In the cooler months of the year, there are numerous frosts and near frosts. Under these dry conditions, the traveller, particularly if accustomed to moist coastal areas, finds a much greater need for fluid intake.

Rainfall is influenced by the various weather systems which affect Australia at different times of the year. During the winter months the South East Trade Winds blow across the northern part of the continent. These winds, which lose their moisture on the east coastal mountains, become dry and sweep across the continent bringing dry conditions. During the summer half of the year, sub-tropical pressure systems move southwards and produce easterly winds across the continent. Between November and April, monsoonal conditions often result in tropical cyclones over the Indian Ocean and Coral Sea; when these approach the coast they produce heavy rains in coastal regions. Sometimes these cyclones produce very strong rain depressions which move inland, producing heavy rains and flooding over wide areas. In Central Australia water soon soaks into the ground and the intense evaporation rapidly dries out the ground surface. These rain depressions are infrequent and irregular, and there may be extended periods, even years, with no rainfall.

The southern part of the continent is under the influence of the westerly prevailing winds from the southern ocean which move northward during the winter period, bringing rainfall to the southern parts of Australia, particularly where they impinge on mountain ranges. As there are no mountains in the southern part of Central Australia the vast area around Lake Eyre has the lowest rainfall in Australia with an average of 125 mm per year or less, with long periods elapsing without rain. Northwards in South Australia, the average rainfall increases to 150 mm per year and for the southern Northern Territory 200 mm per year, reaching 300 mm in the Alice Springs area and northwards.

Finally rainfall in Central Australia is low and unreliable; in the northern parts, it occurs chiefly in summer and particularly during the latter part of the season. Further south, the summer and winter rainfall systems overlap, particularly in autumn; as a result, rainfall, although irregular, may be received at various times of the year. The spring months of September and October may have little or no rainfall.

Topography

The area under discussion is a vast arid region of sandy and stony plains, but also includes some undulating sections with widely spaced rocky outcrops, hills and mountain ranges and numerous sand dunes. These gently sloping plains lie within a series of vast indiscernable drainage basins with a number of shallow, usually dry, river beds and smaller watercourses with extensive flood plains. The large drainage basins are bordered by the hills, mountain ranges and sand dunes. At their lowest points, the basins drain to large salt lakes, numerous playa lakes of salt and clay pans. In the southern part of the area in South Australia, the country east of the Stuart Highway drains to the lowest part of the region around the edges of Lake Eyre. From the lower parts the gently sloping plains rise slowly to the Northern Territory border where the area becomes part of a vast plateau which extends over most of the Northern Territory and Western Australia. This plateau is from 400 to 500 m above sea level, with the central mountain ranges standing from about 300 to 900 m above the plateau.

Landforms

Within the area discussed there are many different landforms: extensive plain areas, which extend for long distances, numerous sand dunes, low undulating hills, rocky outcrops, isolated or groups of rocks, and plateaux projecting above surrounding plains, the remnants of a period many thousands of years ago, when the surrounding country was more elevated. Striking examples of elevated features are Mt Conner, Ayers Rock and the Olgas.

The Plains

Extensive plains are major features of Central Australia, spreading over wide areas, often with imperceptible gentle slopes extending for long distances. The plains are frequently bordered by dissected plateaux, escarpments and sometimes sand dunes; the broad areas between these borders are extensive shallow basins with salt lakes and playa lakes at their low points.

Sandplains

Sandplains are very common and geologists believe that over thousands of years river systems have carried sandstones and other material from the weathering of elevated areas into lower areas or basins. This sand has been spread further by wind action and consequently extensive sandplains have developed.

Daisies growing on a sandplain after rain

Stony or Gibber Plains

In some areas there has been a greater deposition of stony material and silty clays with the sand. Over long periods, winds and other agencies have moved the sand away, leaving behind the heavier stones or gibbers on the ground surfaces, forming stony plains, often called gibber plains. The plains may be extensive and cover wide areas, such as Sturt's Stony Desert. An interesting feature of these gibber plains is that the action of wind over long periods of time has smoothed and polished the surface of the stones, often coating them with a layer of iron oxide which presents a shiny or varnished appearance often referred to as desert varnish.

Sand Dunes

Prevailing winds over thousands of years have in some areas formed sand ridges or dunes which may be quite extensive. Where the winds have blown in the same direction for thousands of years, the dunes have been formed in the direction of the winds. The Simpson Desert is a classical example of this, for innumerable large sand dunes have been formed in almost parallel rows, each extending for many kilometres in a general south to north direction. These dunes are spaced at intervals, sometimes close together, or even a kilometre or more apart, forming distinct flat corridors between dunes which are known as swales. These corridors may have a hard surface of fine silty clays and sand or may be covered with stones as described under stony plains. In other areas where winds blow in different directions, the dunes have formed in various directions and may occur as isolated low to high ridges, or there may be several dunes together without a distinct corridor between. Unlike the moving sands of deserts such as the Sahara, the dunes of Central Australia are generally stabilised on the sides by vegetation, such as saltbush, daisies, pea bushes, cane grass and similar forms of plants.

An interesting feature of the sand dunes is the variation in the colour of the sand. For example, where the dune has been formed of sand which is close to adjoining watercourses and flood plains, or other places where sand is deposited by floodwater, it is chiefly yellowish in colour, which is the general pigmented colour of the quartz from which sand is formed. Where the sand forming the dune has been carried for long distances by the wind over extended periods of time, it

A desolate stony plain
Below: Windblown sand on the top of a dune on Simpson Desert

becomes coated with iron oxide in its passage over the ground, giving the sand a reddish brown colouring. Sand dunes formed by these sands present a reddish brown colour which is characteristic of Central Australia.

The Red Centre

As mentioned under sand dunes, a distinct feature of Central Australia is the reddish brown colour which is due to the widespread presence of iron oxide. Over long periods of time the wind and water have coated the surface of most objects with this iron oxide colouring. Mountain ranges, rocky outcrops and large eminences such as Ayers Rock and the Olgas are coated with it, but where weathered sections of rock break off from the main body, the underlying surface shows the natural colour. Travellers camping in the red sands will find that the ever present red pigment soon stains clothing. Over long periods of time in the northern parts of the area with a higher rainfall, the iron oxide has been dissolved by the water and often deposited in the form of gravels, resulting in the red colouring of objects being less distinct.

Rocky Outcrops, Dissected Plateaux and Escarpments

Throughout the area there are numerous rocky outcrops, from small groups of rocks to rocky hills, escarpments and plateaux which have been worn away or dissected by weathering over long periods of time. These features provide relief to the extensive plain areas and may extend for some distance, or occur as groups or isolated eminences.

Mesas

Amongst the interesting rock forms are the mesas which rise starkly above the surrounding plains. These are remnants of ancient times when the land mass was at a much higher level and the hard nature of their upper surface has resisted weathering. The typical mesa has a flat top formed of hard material called a duricrust; the upper part has vertical sides and the lower part is rugged and sloping, formed from the rock debris which falls with continued weathering. In typical weathering patterns, the rock formation beneath the hard upper crust is softer and weathers at a more rapid rate, so, as it falls away, the upper crust is unsupported and breaks away, adding to the rocky debris below. Mesas may be in groups or isolated; they may be very large, such as Mt Conner, or have weathered to the stage where they are a mere isolated column, for example, Chambers Pillar, a striking rock column situated in the lower south east of the Northern Territory.

Ayers Rock (Uluru) and Mt Olga (Katajuta)

A further example of large striking eminences standing above the surrounding plains is the huge Ayers Rock, the largest monolith in the world, formed of a special type of sandstone known as arkose, which is composed of a mixture of quartz and felspar. An interesting feature of this massive eminence is the vertical manner of the

a   Rocky outcrop, Rainbow Valley
b   A large mesa, Mt Conner
c   A mesa almost worn away, Chambers Pillar
d   Ayers Rock during day
e   Ayers Rock at sunrise

bedding planes of the material from which it is formed. It is believed that there is as much of this huge stone beneath ground as above. Mt Olga, or the Olgas, differs from Ayers Rock and consists of a number of conspicuous, rounded columns grouped together with valleys in between. The material from which these large columns are formed also differs from Ayers Rock as it consists of waterworn stones cemented together by a hard cementing material. This type of formation is known as conglomerate.

Although widely separated, Mt Olga, Ayers Rock and Mt Conner (mentioned under mesas) are all aligned in an east-west direction in the lower south western part of the Northern Territory in the Amadeus Basin, west of the Stuart Highway and readily accessible by road.

A recently published book, *Phanerozoic Earth History of Australia,* considers that the Olgas and Ayers Rock were formed by sediments from the Musgrave Ranges which were once high mountains in the centre of the continent.

a   Sunset, Ayers Rock
b   Ayers Rock wreathed in cloud
c   Water pours off Ayers Rock
d   Texture of Ayers Rock
e   The climbing track Ayers Rock

Above: Mt Olga with Ayers Rock in distance
Below left: Sunset on Mt Olga
Below right: Texture of Mt Olga

The Mountain Ranges

Although vast areas of Central Australia consist of extensive plain country interrupted intermittently by rocky outcrops, dissected plateaux and sand dunes, the mountain ranges of the central area provide some of the most picturesque scenery of Australia. As well as the mountain ranges discussed, there are several small low ranges throughout the area.

Stuart Range

In the southern part of the area near the opal mining town of Coober Pedy is the Stuart Range, a low range of rocky hills situated on the western edge of the Lake Eyre Basin, and extending in a north-south direction for a considerable distance. The Stuart Highway traverses the Stuart Range on its western side.

Everard Range

The Everard Range, with its highest peak, Mt Illbillee, 917 m above sea level, is situated on the western side of the Stuart Highway in the northern part of South Australia, towards the Northern Territory border. On its northern edges the range tends to merge into the Musgrave Ranges.

Musgrave Ranges

The impressive Musgrave Ranges lie in a more or less east-west direction near the South Australian-Northern Territory border, about 300 km south of the town of Alice Springs. These mountain ranges consist of numerous large rounded rocky hills, with some reaching 900 m above the surrounding plains. They do not have a distinct main ridge. The highest peak is Mt Woodruffe, 1439 m above sea level. These mountains are formed of a type of granite called gneiss, different from the rocks of the Macdonnell Ranges which are chiefly sandstone and quartzite. The western end of the Musgrave Ranges adjoins the Petermann Range and the two ranges form the southern edge of the Amadeus Basin, in which basin stand the striking Mt Olga, Ayers Rock and Mt Conner.

Macdonnell Ranges

The Macdonnell Ranges are an extensive group of mountain ranges situated more or less in the centre of Australia. The ranges extend for about 400 km between their eastern and western edges and at their maximum width about 160 km from north to south. The Macdonnells have two main parallel groups of ranges which are formed chiefly of sandstone or hardened sandstone known as quartzite, with some limestone

11

a Parallel ranges in Macdonnell Ranges
b Ridges in Macdonnell Ranges
c The Chewing Range
d Harts Range
e Central Mt Stuart

ridges. In the southern group of ranges, the James Range in the east adjoins the Krichauff Range and then the George Gill Range in the west. The southern side of the three ranges forms the northern boundary of the Amadeus Basin whilst on the northern side of the ranges are the Missionary plains.

The northern group of ranges has the highest mountains in Central Australia, the highest being Mt Liebig, 1524 m above sea level, closely followed by Mt Zeil, 1510 m above sea level. Mt Sonder, although of lesser height, 1380 m, is better known and more accessible. These northern ranges are dominated by the Chewing Range in the west and the Waterhouse Range in the south east. On the north east, the Macdonnells extend into the Harts Range, which borders the northern edge of the Simpson Desert. The north side of the Macdonnells forms the edge of the Burt Plain.

The Macdonnell Ranges are dissected by numerous valleys and gorges which make the ranges a place of unlimited scenic beauty. The town of Alice Springs is situated within the eastern part of the Macdonnell Ranges, with the southern entrance to the town through a distinctive gap known as Heavitree Gap. Through this gap pass the Todd River, the Stuart Highway and the railway line.

Northern Ranges

North of the Macdonnell Ranges and to the west of the Stuart Highway are several groups of low mountain ranges. Stuart Bluff, the Reynolds, Mt Doreen and Truer Ranges form the northern edge of Burt Plain. The Reynolds Range, on its north side, merges with Central Mt Stuart, the approximate central point of Australia. North and west of these ranges there are rocky outcrops, such as the Granites, an old goldmining site, which is on the border of the Tanami Desert. Adjoining the Stuart Highway lies the Barrow Creek Uplift, a group of low

rocky hills, near the small settlement of Barrow Creek. The last group of ranges, the Davenport-Murchison Ranges, are situated in a north-west direction, with the northern edges of the range being traversed by the Stuart Highway. Associated with the edge of the Davenport-Murchison Ranges, midway between Barrow Creek and Tennant Creek, are the unique Devil's Marbles, which are a number of superimposed large rounded granite boulders.

a   Devils Marbles
b   Lake Eyre filled with water
c   A typical claypan — Simpson Desert
d   A salt lake after rain — Lake Hart

Playas, Claypans, Saltlakes and Saltpans

Throughout the area there are numerous shallow depressions in drainage basins and plain areas. The almost flat depressions may extend over wide areas and after heavy rains hold water and appear as lakes. With the high evaporation rate, the water soon disappears, leaving a clayey, salty or gypsoferous (gypsum — calcium sulphate) deposit on the bottom or floor of the depression. These shallow depressions are known as playas and, depending upon the nature of the material deposited, various common names are applied to them, e.g. claypans, saltpans or saltlakes (salinas). These playas occur in greatest number north of Lake Eyre on the Simpson Desert, between the top of the lake and the South Australian, Northern Territory and Queensland border at a spot known as Poepples Corner. There are hundreds of clay-pans and salinas between the sand dunes, from small to large and of various shapes.

Claypans

Over the millenia fine silty clays, often dissolved as minute particles in the water, have been deposited in the depressions, building up successive layers of fine clays. This fine clayey material cracks extensively when dry, which permits air circulation, followed by drying out of the soil and roots of plants. Claypans are commonly bereft of perennial vegetation, but sometimes there may be coarse woody perennial shrubs such as lignum or saltbush present. Generally the vegetation is of an ephemeral or annual nature.

Saltpans, Saltlakes, Salinas

In many areas, various types of salts are dissolved from rocks, such as different forms of calcium (lime and gypsum), common salt (sodium chloride), salts of magnesium (magnesium sulphate — Epsom salts). The salts are carried in solution in water and, as the water

evaporates, crystallise out within the soil or may form a white deposit on the surface. Over the ages this process has continued and the salts deposited may be thick; in other cases the salt layer on the surface is only a thin skin, but still gives the appearance of a salt lake. Lake Eyre is a large deep lake and, over millions of years, salts of various types have been deposited, building up a thick layer, but even at Lake Eyre there is a mixture of both salts and clays. Some salt lakes have a pink appearance, which occurs when a special form of bacteria grows on the surface of the salt. Plants do not grow in the bed of salt lakes, but specialised plants such as samphires, saltbush and other salt tolerant bushes may grow around the margins.

Mound Springs

The north-eastern corner of South Australia and the lower corner of south-eastern Northern Territory are on the western edge of the Great Artesian Basin. This huge underground basin extends over a large part of western Queensland and north west New South Wales, as well as the areas mentioned above. Bores are drilled into this huge underground reservoir to provide water for cattle. Unfortunately most of the water from the Artesian Basin has a high content of various salts which renders it undrinkable for humans.

An interesting feature of the lower part of the Oodnadatta area are the Mound Springs which are

natural outlets for water from the Artesian basin. With the evaporation of the water, the dissolved salts combine with sand and, over a long period, form a ring or mound around the escaping water, creating a pond from which water seeps away into the surrounding sands. In some areas where the soil is less impervious, the flow from the spring may be of sufficient volume to allow a swamp to develop.

Dalhousie Springs

One of the most remarkable groups of springs is an area known as Dalhousie Springs in the far north-eastern part of South Australia, near the Northern Territory border and the edge of the Simpson Desert. In this otherwise barren and stony region there are dozens of springs spread over an extensive area; they form oases, each spring being surrounded by paperbark trees, saltbush and other plants. Unlike most mound springs, some of the Dalhousie springs have good drinking water. This area is unfortunately well removed from tourist roads; formerly a cattle station, it was recently acquired by the

a Dalhousie Springs
b A mound spring
c Part of Amadeus Basin

South Australian Government for a National Park to preserve the unique nature of the area.

A further large gushing spring is located in the Simpson Desert between sand dunes and is known as Purni Bore. Large volumes of very hot, almost boiling, water flow to the surface and, with the soil being somewhat impervious, a permanent lake has formed with various types of water plants growing around the margins, and a range of waterbirds. Unfortunately the water is not drinkable.

The Drainage Basins

Lake Eyre Basin

The Lake Eyre Basin is one of the largest drainage basins in the world, extending over a vast area. It includes the north-eastern part of South Australia, the south-east part of the Northern Territory, extends northwards to the Barkly Tablelands and covers a large part of Western Queensland. The lowest point of the basin is Lake Eyre, a huge salt lake with a mixture of salt and silt. It has a larger northern part and smaller southern section, and is 14 m below sea level at its lowest point. There are innumerable playa lakes and smaller salt lakes within the basin. The large inland rivers of western Queensland and the south eastern rivers of the Northern Territory and north-west South Australia flow into the Lake Eyre Basin. Although these huge river systems bring massive volumes of water into the basin during wet seasons, it is only when there is intensive rainfall for several wet seasons in succession that there is sufficient flow to fill Lake Eyre. it is believed that the lake only fills with water two or three times in a century, as the water is usually lost in desert sands, flood plains and playa lakes.

Amadeus Basin

The Amadeus Basin is a vast shallow indiscernable desert basin with extensive sandplains and innumerable

sand dunes. The basin drains westwards into two large salt lakes, Lake Amadeus and Lake Neale. The southern boundary of the basin is formed by the Musgrave and Petermann Ranges whilst the southern part of the Macdonnell Ranges in the form of the Krichauff, James and George Gill Ranges provide the northern boundary of the basin. On its eastern edge the Amadeus Basin adjoins the Lake Eyre Basin which is represented in this part by the Henbury-Eldunda Plain. Within the southern part of the Amadeus basin stand three well known features, Mt Conner, Ayers Rock and the Olgas. These three large emminences, although widely separated, are aligned in an east-west direction.

Missionary Plain

This long narrow plain which drains into the Finke River and its tributaries is situated within the Macdonnell Ranges, bounded on the south by the Krichauff, James and George Gill Ranges and on the north by the Chewing and Macdonnell Ranges. A well developed road system through this plain provides ready access to the many scenic points of the Macdonnell Ranges.

Burt Plain

North of the Macdonnell Ranges is a further gently sloping basin known as Burt Plain, which drains westward into the salt lake, Lake Bennett. The basin is bounded on the north and east by the Mt Doreen, Gruer and Reynolds Ranges.

Tanami Basin

North of the Mt Doreen and Reynolds Ranges, the country passes through rocky outcrops into a vast sandy basin known as the Tanami desert, with wide sandy plains.

Sandover Plenty Plains

The Sandover Plenty Plains drain into the Sandover and Plenty rivers which drain eastwards to the Georgina River and southwards to the Simpson desert. In the south, the area is bounded by the Macdonnell-Harts Ranges and in the north by the Davenport Murchison Ranges, north east of Tennants Creek. The rocky Barrow Hills or Uplift form the western boundary of the plains. A most unusual feature adjoining the Stuart Highway on the western boundary of the Sandover Plains is a group of very large rounded granite boulders known as the Devil's Marbles. A further interesting point south of the small settlement of Barrow Creek and slightly west of the Stuart Highway is Central Mount Stuart, representing the true centre of Australia. In a broad sense, the Sandover Plenty Plains form part of the vast Georgina basin.

The River Systems

Central Australia does not have any rivers which flow continuously; for the greater part of the time, the water-courses are merely dry channels. Along the beds of the larger water-courses there are occasional waterholes,

a Part of Missionary Plains
b Part of Burt Plain
c Tanami Track

some of which may be fed by springs and persist, even during extended dry periods. Much of the area through which the rivers pass is very flat. The river channels may be distinct in parts, but frequently spread out into wide shallow waterways and, in parts, may be in the form of flood plains with indistinguishable channels. During periods of extended rains the watercourses may be many kilometres wide, with numerous indefinite waterways, flooding vast areas of the Lake Eyre basin which become impassable.

A feature of the watercourses which pass through arid areas lacking in perennial vegetation, is the presence of trees and shrubs along the banks or in the beds of the watercourse. On larger rivers with deeper soils and underground moisture, eucalyptus trees, commonly known as river gums, and coolabahs are present, together with smaller trees and shrubs, such as paperbarks, mulga, emu bush, saltbush and the like. On flood plains in lower areas of watercourses, where the soil has sufficient underground moisture and is not subject to cracking, coolabahs, acàcia such as gidgee,

a   A permanent waterhole on the Diamantina River near Birdsville
b   A waterhole in bed of Coopers Creek
c   Coopers Creek in flood
d   Mt Sonder and Finke River

paperbarks and other shrubs such as lignum are common. Small coolabah, paperbarks, mulga and smaller shrubs occur along the banks of small watercourses where less moisture is available.

The North and Eastern Rivers
Diamantina, Georgina and Mulligan Rivers

These rivers which arise in western Queensland and in the north eastern Northern Territory, with their numerous tributaries, carry vast volumes of water during summer monsoonal rains. Although the rivers flow into the vast Lake Eyre Basin, they do not have distinct continuous channels into Lake Eyre. The Diamantina River discharges on to vast flood plains and the extensive spreading Goyders Lagoon or Swamp, north west of Lake Eyre. During extended wet periods, when the whole area becomes saturated, water from the flood plains flows into the Warburton River or Creek, carrying floodwaters into Lake Eyre.

The Georgina, which rises in the Barkly Tableland in the north eastern Northern Territory, has its associated tributaries in western Queensland and, during monsoonal rains, with the more southern Mulligan River, discharges its large volume of water on to vast flood plains at the edge of the Simpson Desert, where the water is lost in the desert sands. With extended wet periods and recurrent wet seasons, the areas become saturated and water may reach Lake Eyre through the shallow watercourses of Eyre's Creek and Kallakoopah River.

Coopers Creek

Although named Coopers Creek by Captain Charles Sturt, Coopers Creek or The Cooper is a river in the true sense. It may be a dry river bed with an occasional waterhole for most of the time, but, with its main tributaries, the Thompson and Barcoo Rivers, collects large volumes of water from south western Queensland during heavy monsoonal rains. For some of its way Coopers Creek has a fairly distinct water channel, but, like the other rivers, in its low part spreads over wide flood plains, requiring extended rains to flow into Lake Eyre.

The North Eastern Rivers
Finke River

This large river which commences in the western Macdonnell Ranges with its main tributaries, the Palmer and Hugh Rivers, flows through deep gorges and wide sandy channels in the Macdonnell Ranges. There are a number of permanent waterholes fed by springs in the bed of the river. In the flatter areas towards the Northern Territory — South Australian border, the river channel becomes wider and shallower and, in South Australia on the south-western edge of the Simpson Desert, the river spreads out into broad channels and vast flood plains. During extended periods of rain the flood waters make their way into the broad Macumba River, and ultimately into Lake Eyre when wet seasons persist.

Todd, Hale, Plenty and Hay Rivers

These rivers which commence in the eastern Macdonnell-Harts Range are dry channels for most of the time. The broad shallow dry sandy bed of the Todd River with its large River Gums and which extends through the town of Alice Springs is typical. During periods of extended heavy rains, these rivers, which flow south-east, discharge their water into the desert sands of the northern part of the Simpson Desert.

Sandover River

This river which rises from the northern side of the Macdonnell-Harts Range flows eastwards towards the Northern Territory — Queensland border and during periods of extended rains spreads into flood plains near the borders, the floodwaters eventually making their way into the Georgina River system.

The South Western Rivers

Macumba River

This river, with its main tributaries, the Hamilton and Alberga Rivers, becomes wide, shallow and spreading in the flat country above Lake Eyre and collects water from the flood plains of the Finke River during periods of extended heavy rains, with the water ultimately reaching Lake Eyre.

The Neales

Commencing in the hills on the edge of the Lake Eyre Basin west of Oodnadatta, the Neales, with a main north and south branch and several southern tributaries, becomes broad and shallow in the flat country through which it passes in its eastward path to Lake Eyre. Although a dry bed for most of the time, it soon becomes impassable after heavy rains.

The Southern Watercourses

South of the Neales, there are a number of small watercourses which arise in the Stuart Range and surrounding area and then flow to a shallow salt lake in the northern part. The southern waterways make their way to Lake Eyre South. As this is the most arid part of the area discussed, the waterways are merely shallow, dry watercourses most of the time.

a Finke River in Macdonnell Ranges
b Finke River near its flood plain brings sand to add to dunes and sand plains
c Dry bed of the Todd River near Alice Springs

Access to the Area

There is a railway line providing direct access to Alice Springs and settlements en route and also an air service. Road access to the general area is limited due to its difficult nature and the small size and number of settlements. With the search for oil in recent years, numbers of roughly formed exploration tracks have been made to provide access to uninhabitable areas. These tracks are not maintained, with the result that, when oil surveys are completed, they soon fall into disrepair with sand drifting over them. With the development of the Moomba gas and oil fields, situated in the north east corner of South Australia, ready access is now available to this limited area.

There are few properly formed roads in the area and, generally a four-wheel drive vehicle is required for most tracks. Without advising proper authorities, venturing from established roads and tracks is inadvisable.

Roads and Tracks

Stuart Highway

The Stuart Highway is the only direct access road from Port Augusta in southern Australia to the city of Darwin in the far north, a distance of about 2900 km. Enroute the road passes through numerous small settlements and the town of Alice Springs. To give some idea of the

a New Glendambo Roadhouse, Stuart Highway
b Part of the Birdsville Track
c Eastern end of Plenty River Road
d One millionth sleeper of new railway line
e Mine shaft Roxby Downs

vastness of the area discussed, the distance from the southern point near Woomera in South Australia to the town of Tennant Creek in the Northern Territory is about 1500 km. Extensive realignment and sealing of the highway which skirts the western edge of the Lake Eyre Basin has been carried out and is in continuous progress, ultimately resulting in a sealed road to Alice Springs, joining the already sealed road to Darwin.

With the upgrading of the highway, a new roadhouse and settlement have been built at Glendambo, 163 km from Woomera. A further roadhouse and settlement have been developed at Marla, adjoining the old Marla Bore, on a new railway siding approximately 140 km from the South Australian — Northern Territory border and serving the areas formerly serviced by the old Ghan Railway.

Port Augusta-Maree Road

This part-sealed road, which more or less followed the old Port Augusta — Alice Springs railway, extends for a distance of 377 km. The roadway skirts the western edge of the Flinders Range and passes through several small towns.

Maree — Oodnadatta — Granite Downs Tracks

This secondary road and track proceeds north-west along the route of the old railway, skirting Lake Eyre, then south through an area subject to flooding and continues for a distance of about 380 km to the small town of Oodnadatta, a central point in the area. On this section a number of mound springs are passed. From Oodnadatta the track proceeds in a westerly direction to join the Stuart Highway, west of a station property known as Granite Downs, and near the new settlement of Marla.

Maree — Birdsville Track

This track, which commences at Maree, extends for 483 km to the small settlement of Birdsville, situated in far western Queensland on the Diamantina River, near the South Australian border, east of the Simpson Desert. The track skirts the eastern edge of Lake Eyre, the western edge of the Strzelecki Desert and Sturts Stony Desert, crossing sandplains, stony plains, sand dunes and claypans. At the Maree end of the track Coopers Creek and its floodplains are crossed. In the north at Clifton Hills, the track divides into an inner and outer track, the old inside track crossing part of the vast floodout of the Diamantina River, known as Goyder's

Lagoon. The outer or dry weather track skirts the outer edge of the floodplain and has become the regularly maintained track, crossing the Diamantina River near Birdsville.

From Birdsville an unsealed secondary road travels north-wards along the eastern edge of the Simpson Desert to the small towns of Bedourie and Boulia from where a sealed road extends north to the town of Mt Isa and eastwards to the town of Winton. Westwards a dirt track joins the Plenty River Road at the Queensland — Northern Territory border.

A further road from Birdsville travels eastwards more or less along the Queensland — South Australian border to the towns of Betoota and Windorah.

Plenty River and Sandover Roads

Some 70 km north of Alice Springs, the Plenty River Road branches off the Stuart Highway and extends eastwards to the Northern Territory — Queensland border, from where a track leads to the town of Boulia, the road skirting the Harts Range and traversing flat plain areas with numerous small water courses associated with the Plenty River. The road is impassable after rains. A short distance after leaving the Stuart Highway, the Sandover Road branches off and extends eastwards along the Sandover River with its flood plains. Like the Plenty River Road, the Sandover Road is impassable after rain.

Halls Creek — Tanami Desert Track

About 20 km north of Alice Springs a road branches off the Stuart Highway and extends in a north west direction. It finally becomes the Tanami Track, traversing the Tanami Desert into Western Australia and Halls Creek.

Mt Isa Highway

A few kilometres north of Tennant Creek the main Mt Isa — Barkly Highway branches off the Stuart Highway. This sealed road traverses the Barkly Tableland.

Track from Queensland border to Innamincka and Strzelecki Track

From the Queensland border a track extends southwards along the edge of Sturt's Stony Desert through the old station property of Cordello Downs, continuing south to the small settlement of Innamincka, situated on Coopers Creek.

From Innamincka the unsealed Strzelecki Track follows the direction of Strzelecki Creek to the Moomba/Gidgealpa Oil and Gas Field. A network of roads radiating in different directions has been developed around the Field, with the old Strzelecki Track travelling south west to Lyndhurst on the Port Augusta — Maree Road. About 60 km south of Moomba, a road leaves the Strzelecki Track and travels in a south easterly direction to Cameron's Corner at the junction of the Queensland, South Australian and New South Wales borders.

Yulara — Ayers Rock — Mt Olga Road

About 230 km south of Alice Springs and 70 km north of the small settlement of Kulgera near the Northern Territory — South Australian border, a sealed road leaves the Stuart Highway at Eridunda, where a new roadhouse has been built. The sealed road goes westwards to the new village and airport of Yulara about 240 km from the Stuart Highway. From Yulara, the road serves Ayers Rock about 20 km away and Mt Olga about 30 km. To the west of the Olgas lie the Petermann Ranges, Western Australian border, and Gibson and Great Victoria Deserts, to which there is restricted access.

Alice Springs Roads

Extending from the town of Alice Springs are a number of sealed and unsealed roads leading in various directions, providing ready access to the numerous tourist attractions and stations in the surrounding area, as shown in Map 2.

Rail Access

The area is served by a new standard gauge railway line which is provided with new modern rolling stock. The new railway line leaves the transcontinental railway line at the settlement of Tarcoola, to terminate at Alice Springs. En route several sidings have been provided to serve the surrounding settlements. The new rail line follows a more direct route than the old line and has been built on higher ground to avoid flooding. At Alice Springs goods for northern parts, including Darwin, must be transhipped and carried northwards by road transport; large trucks with several trailing waggons are used for large loads and are known as road trains.

The old railway was known as the 'Ghan' and was associated with the early development of South Australia and the Northern Territory. The line was built in stages as development occurred over an extended period. The small town of Maree was the terminus of the line for many years and camels were used to transport goods to surrounding areas. The camel drivers were Afghans from whom the name of the old train was taken. The train line was next extended to Oodnadatta which was the terminus for some years, and finally to Alice Springs. The old line passed through low lying areas subject to flooding, the route to some extent being determined by availability of water for the steam locomotives, which was obtained from the conveniently situated mound springs. With the closure of the old line, there was little need for a number of the small settlements which developed, so some of them have been deserted and are now derelict.

The old line is still maintained to Maree, as open cut mining for coal is carried out at Leigh Creek, south of Maree.

Towns

The whole area is sparsely populated with small settlements and a number of roadhouses with stores along the Stuart Highway and the Port Augusta — Oodnatta Road. The towns are listed from the southern part of the area in South Australia, along the Stuart Highway to Tennant Creek in the Northern Territory. In the east the towns are listed northwards from Maree in South Australia.

Andamooka

This is a small opal mining settlement, north of the town of Woomera and some 100 km east of the Stuart Highway. Having grown as opal mining developed, with buildings being erected adjoining mining sites, there has not been much order in layout. With open cut mining now in use and on a larger scale, the town is developing in a more orderly manner, with general shopping facilities available. With the nearby Roxby Downs uranium, gold

and copper mine providing employment, the town will grow more rapidly. The nearby Olympic Downs Village has been built to house workers at Roxby Downs.

Coober Pedy

This large opal field has been in operation for many years; the temporary phase of the town has long passed and there are now hotels, stores of different types and a modern hospital. One great problem is lack of water, as there is no source of water in the area and all supplies have to be carted. Coober Pedy is in one of the most arid parts of Australia.

Alice Springs

The town of Alice Springs, situated on the eastern part of the Macdonnell Ranges, slightly south of the true centre of 'Australia, is the focal point of some of the most striking and scenic features in Australia. Within a radius of 200 to 300 km there are numerous places to visit, including such well known features as Ayers Rock and Palm Valley. Alice Springs is a rapidly developing town, with modern shopping complexes and hotels, art galleries, an airport and even a modern gambling casino. Situated at the end of the railway line where all goods must be transhipped to travel northwards, Alice Springs is a thriving town, providing all the facilities for the surrounding properties and settlements, as well as the tourist trade.

Tennant Creek

This well established town with shopping facilities is a centre for large gold and copper mining operations. It is also a centre for the surrounding area and, being situated near the junction of the Stuart Highway and Mt Isa — Barkly Highway, goods can be readily transported to and from South Australia and Queensland.

Maree

This town is once more the terminus for the railway from Port Augusta, since the abandonment of the 'Ghan' railway line to Alice Springs. As well as serving as a railway terminus, this small town provides shopping facilities, is a supply centre for cattle properties in the area and extending to Birdsville in Queensland, and provides facilities for transporting cattle to Port Augusta.

a   Part of Andamooka town and opal workings
b   Catacomb Church in an old opal mine Coober Pedy
c   Opal workings Coober Pedy
d   Todd Street, a main street in Alice Springs
e   Road train and bus — transport between
    Darwin and Alice Springs

Oodnadatta

This town is no longer served by a railway since the abandonment of the line from Maree to Alice Springs. However, with its shopping facilities, it still serves as a centre for the area, being supplied by road from Maree and Marla on the new Alice Springs railway. It has a large aboriginal population.

Birdsville

This town, situated in Queensland near the South Australian border, is on the Diamantina River, where there are permanent waterholes. The town is a centre for surrounding station properties, has general shopping facilities and serves as a focal point for the more adventurous tourist, as it is situated on the eastern side of the Simpson Desert and is conveniently located for light aircraft travelling in the centre of the continent. Birdsville supports an annual race meeting which attracts many visitors.

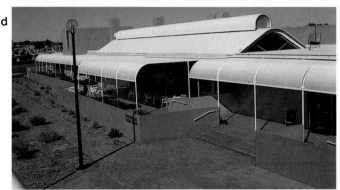

Ayers Rock Resort—Yulara

Considerable development has occurred in the area with every facility for the tourist visiting Ayers Rock, Mt Olga and the surrounding area. A small township has been developed, centred on the large Ayers Rock Resort with two first class hotels, the modern Red Centre Motel, a gorup of cabins, dormitory accommodation and a large camping ground. There is a modern shopping complex, a theatre, visitors centre, a tavern, a service station and an airport.

a   Old residence and new Post Office, Alice Springs
b   Gas separators, Moomba Oilfield
c   Old Telegraph Station, Alice Springs
d   Entrance to Ayers Rock Resort
e   Post Office, Maree
f   Hotel Birdsville with airport adjoining
g   Flynn Memorial

21

a

Simpson Desert Crossing

Plates *a* to *i* were taken during the first crossing of the Simpson Desert by a large passenger bus in August 1983, which took five days, including a delay of 24 hours when overnight rain prevented movement on a claypan. The high evaporation rate discussed under 'Climate' completely dried the claypan within 24 hours. Although the bus was equipped with special wide tyres and metal tracks were used to mount the higher dunes, the long wheelbase of the bus caused the vehicle to bottom on the crests of high dunes. This necessitated the physical removal of many tonnes of sand from dune crests. On one occasion this amounted to 600 tonnes.

a Dalhousie Springs, the last available drinking water, with sign to Birdsville
b Looking across some closely arranged dunes
c Purni Bore near the western edge of the Simpson, a bore made into the Great Artesian Basin many years ago for cattle; water is undrinkable by humans
d Bus stuck on top of a dune crest
e A drifting dune across an existing track
f Top of dune being removed
g The only eucalypt (a coolibah) in the Simpson Desert
h Bus passing through water in a section of Goyders Lagoon on the eastern side of the Simpson
i The eastern side of the Simpson Desert, adjoining the Birdsville Track
j Standley Chasm
k Simpsons Gap
l Palm Valley
m Glen Helen Gorge
n Kings Canyon

b

c

d

e

22

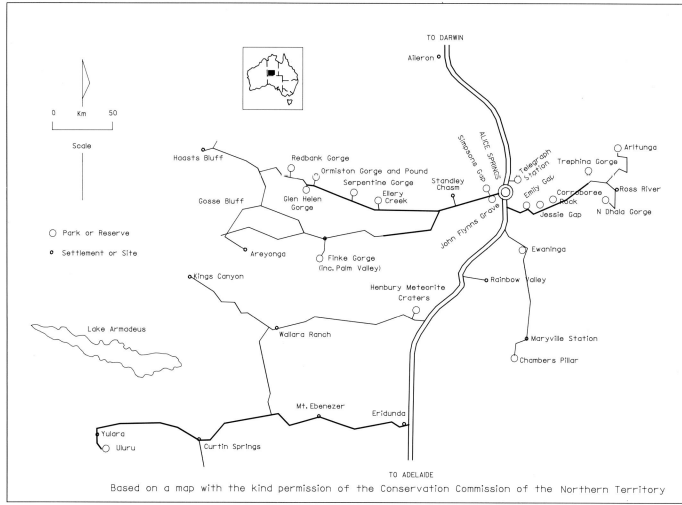

TO DARWIN

Aileron

ALICE SPRINGS

Simpsons Gap

Haasts Bluff
Redbank Gorge
Ormiston Gorge and Pound
Serpentine Gorge
Standley Chasm
Telegraph Station
Trephina Gorge
Arltunga
Glen Helen Gorge
Ellery Creek
Emily Gap
Corroboree Rock
Ross River
Gosse Bluff
Jessie Gap
N Dhala Gorge
John Flynns Grave
Areyonga
Finke Gorge (inc. Palm Valley)
Ewaninga
Kings Canyon
Rainbow Valley
Henbury Meteorite Craters
Lake Armadeus
Wallara Ranch
Maryville Station
Chambers Pillar
Mt. Ebenezer
Eridunda
Yulara
Uluru
Curtin Springs

TO ADELAIDE

0 Km 50
Scale

○ Park or Reserve
○ Settlement or Site

Based on a map with the kind permission of the Conservation Commission of the Northern Territory

These pages will enable you to select and find your way to any of twenty three central Australian parks and reserves.

Once there, don't expect to see euros, dingoes and other shy wildlife at every step. Timing your walks for early morning or late afternoon will help, but make sure you allow plenty of time to soak up everything these areas have to offer. Allow yourself time to wander or sit quietly and take in the sounds, smells and feelings that surround you.

Road conditions

For certain parks four wheel drive (4WD) are recommended, as access is via rough tracks which are commonly impassable to conventional vehicles. Once in the park, such vehicles must of course remain on roadways.

Wet weather will affect road surfaces and rising creeks can cut roadways, leaving motorists stranded. However, advice on current road conditions is available through Northern Territory Emergency Services, Telephone Alice Springs 52 3833.

Water

Where available, park water comes from natural supplies which are not treated to meet recognised health standards. Visitors should therefore carry their own supply of drinking water.

How you can help

Leave your pets at home. Dogs can foul barbecue and camping areas and annoy other visitors. Lost cats survive and can wipe out the area's smaller native animals.

Drive only on roadways. Each visitor driving off roadways adds to wildlife destruction by wrecking burrows, changing the grass cover and encouraging wind and water erosion.

The system of parks and reserves

The Conservation Commission administers five categories of land whose purpose is to preserve the Territory's natural and cultural features.

1. **National Parks** are large, unspoilt nature conservation areas managed with minimal interference and permanently available for public enjoyment, education and inspiration.

2. **Nature Parks** are smaller natural areas also set aside for public appreciation but whose management allows for the provision of more amenities.

3. **Conservation Reserves** aim to protect features of particular scientific value.

4. **Historical Reserves** preserve sites of significant historical value.

5. **Game Reserves** are for the maintenance of game, some of which can be harvested under permit.

Parks and Reserves of Central Australia

NAME	FEATURES	Kilometres from Alice Springs (*4WD recommended)	Area (hectares)	Camping allowed	Picnic facilities	Wood B.B.Q.	Gas B.B.Q.	Toilets
North (via Stuart Highway)								
1. Alice Springs Telegraph Station Historical Reserve	Restored site of first European settlement, walking tracks.	5	445		•	•	•	•
2. Central Mount Stuart Historical Reserve	Memorial to explorer John McDouall Stuart.	216	0.3					
3. Devils Marbles Conservation Reserve	Piles of huge granite boulders.	393	1 823	•	•			•
4. John Flynn's Historical Reserve	Monument to a founder of the Flying Doctor Service.	529	0.5		•			
5. Attack Creek Historical Reserve	Memorial to where, in 1860, John McDouall Stuart's northward expedition was turned back by hostile Aboriginals.				•			
South (via Old South Road)								
1. Ewaninga Rock Carvings Reserve	Prehistoric rock carvings.	39	6		•	•		•
2. Chamber's Pillar Historical Reserve	Historic sandstone pillar bearing dates and names of early explorers and pastoralists.	165*	340	•	•	•		
South West (via Stuart Highway)								
1. Henbury Meteorite Conservation Reserve	Twelve meteorite craters, the largest being 180 metres wide.	147	16	•	•	•		•
2. Uluru (Ayers Rock — Mt Olga) National park	World's largest monolith; sandhill and plains country, domes of the Olgas; Visitor Centre.	470	126 132	•	•	•		•
3. Rainbow Valley	Attractive rock outcroppings	98			•			
East (via Ross Highway)								
1. Emily and Jessie Gap Nature Park	Two rocky gaps in the MacDonnell Ranges with semi-permanent water.	13	695	•	•	•		•
2. Corroboree Rock Conservation Reserve	Rocky outcrop used by early Aborigines.	48	7	•	•	•		•
3. Trephina Gorge Nature Park	Ranges scenery; sandy creek and waterholes.	85	1 771	•	•	•	•	•
4. N'Dhala Gorge Nature Park	Prehistoric rock engravings in rugged gorge.	98	501	•	•	•		•
5. Arltunga Historical Reserve	Ruins of goldfield settlement; graves; restored gaol, mineshafts and battery site.	111	4 893	•	•	•		•
West (via Larapinta Drive)								
1. John Flynn's Grave Historical Reserve	Monument and grave of Flying Doctor Service founder.	7	0.3		•			
2. Simpson's Gap National Park	Scenic gaps and ranges; rock wallabies; Visitor Centre.	18	30 950		•		•	•
3. Ellery Creek Big Hole Nature Park	Large waterhole and gap.	93	1 776	•	•	•		•
4. Serpentine Gorge Nature Park	Ranges scenery; narrow, watered gorges.	104	518			•		•
5. Ormiston Gorge and Pound National Park	Large rugged gorge; waterhole and enclosed valley.	132	4 655	•	•	•	•	•
6. Glen Helen Gorge Nature Park	Scenic rock formation where Finke River cuts MacDonnell Ranges.	133	386					
7. Redbank Nature Park	Red-walled gorge and permanent water.	161	1 295	•	•			•
8. Finke Gorge National Park	Finke River; wilderness areas; rugged landforms; Palm Valley's ancient plant life.	155*	45 856	•	•	•	•	•

Courtesy: Conservation Commission of the Northern Territory.

a   Gosses Bluff
b   Saltbush in the bottom of a meteorite crater
c   Trephina Gorge, eastern Macdonnells
d   Corroboree Rock
e   Ormiston Gorge
f   Kings Canyon Valley

Flora

Many forms of Australian plants have evolved to withstand dry conditions and in Central Australia the vegetation is particularly adapted to the arid conditions of the area. Leaves generally present their edges to the sunlight, and are often tough, leathery and thickened, terminating in a stiff point, or small and needle-like; alternatively they may be thick, fleshy and succulent, enabling water to be stored. The surfaces of the leaves and stems are often coated with a waxy varnish-like substance which makes them shiny, or with a whitish, greyish bloom, or a dense covering of fine downy hairs. The presentation of the leaf edges to the sunlight and the variety of surface coatings have the effect of reducing transpiration loss of moisture to a minimum. Further, the plants develop deep root systems which enable them to obtain moisture from lower soil levels, as surface moisture is rapidly evaporated, as discussed under 'Climate'.

Nature of Plants

A further adaptation to arid conditions is in the very nature of the plants, for example, some plants are able to die back to the roots and remain in this state until rain or adequate moisture is received. Typical examples of this are the Rock Ferns (*Cheilanthes*), the unusual Nardoo Fern (*Marsilea*) and others such as the perennial grasses, eg. *Aristida.* Where the moisture in the soil is insufficient to support plant growth throughout the year, plants which have a short life cycle are the dominant types. Such plants are able to germinate rapidly from seed, grow quickly and flower, produce seed and then die, repeating the process when suitable conditions prevail, which may be several years later. This form of plant is known as an annual or ephemeral and includes daisies, grasses, many pea flowers and the like. Where

the soil moisture is sufficient to support plants throughout the year, there are various types of succulent plants, shrubs and trees which may live for many years. These plants are known as perennials and include members of the Saltbush Family (Chenpodiaceae), Emu Bush *(Eremophila)*, cassias, *Acacia* (wattles), eucalypts and many other types of plants. During extended dry periods these perennial type plants may drop their leaves to reduce the transpiration of moisture and in long lasting droughts may even die. After rains many types of annuals grow amongst the existing plant communities.

Nature of Soil

Apart from the availability of moisture, the nature of the soil has a considerable influence on the type of plants that grow in a particular area. Many forms of plants will only grow on particular types of soil, whilst others are more adaptable and grow on different soil types. Central Australia has many different types of soil. Some of the more common types are:
(1) Sandy soils; these usually have varying proportions of fine clay intermixed and are known as sandy loams.
(2) The soil may be stony with large stones intermixed with smaller stones, sand and other materials.
(3) Soil may be of a heavy nature with a large proportion of clay, or it may be derived from different forms of lime or calcium (known as calcareous soils) which are of a heavy clayey type.
(4) In shallow depressions such as playa lakes the soil may be of very finely grained clay and form large areas known as claypans which develop large cracks when dry.
(5) Frequently the soil may have a salt content and is known as saline soil.

Other Factors Influencing Plant Growth

The depth of soil, its moisture holding capacity and freedom from cracking when dry, its susceptibility to regular flooding, as in the case of floodplains of watercourses, all have considerable influence on plant growth.

The shade and protection provided by gullies and valleys in eroded plateaux, escarpments and mountain ranges, produce environments less harsh than more open areas. Under these more favourable conditions, plants which are unable to exist under the surrounding harsh conditions may be able to develop. Two examples of such plant growth are, the cycad, *Macrozamia macdonnellii,* and the Cabbage Palm, *Livistona mariae,* both of which are restricted to protected and partly shaded gullies and valleys of the Macdonnell Ranges.

Watercourses, although dry for most of the time, may contain moisture at some depth below the bed of the water channel. This available moisture may enable larger trees to grow in the river bed and along the edges of the watercourse. Eucalypts, such as River Gums and coolabah, may be present, and others such as paperbarks, wattles and the like, may grow along the banks, even though the surrounding area may be bereft of vegetation.

Hibiscus or Mallow Family Malvaceae

This large family is widely distributed, particularly in the tropical parts of the world and consists of herbs, shrubs to small trees, frequently with rough lobed leaves and small or large flowers. In addition to the native species, two exotic genera, each with one species, are naturalised in the area; these are *Malva parviflora* and *Malvastrum americanum.* The commercial cotton is obtained from one of the exotic *Gossypium* species.

Hibiscus

It is not generally realised that there are a number of native Australian *Hibiscus,* with about ten species in the area. Flowers occur singly and the style is branched into 5 lobes at the apex; there are 5 calyx lobes and a further ring of bracts around the calyx, known as an epicalyx, which has from 5 to 12 lobes, rarely 5; the seed capsule has 5 chambers. One of the species, *H. sturtii,* with a number of varieties is widely distributed.

H. sturtii A small shrub 0.5 to 1 m high; leaves whitish to greyish green, egg-shaped to oblong/ lance-shaped, with or without coarse toothing; flowers white to pink with a red coloured centre. Occurs on sandy and gravelly soils and rocky slopes.

Radyera

There are two species in this genus, one in South Africa and the other in the drier parts of Australia. It differs from *Hibiscus* in that the flowers grow in clusters, the apex of the style is enlarged but not divided, and there are 10 chambers in the seed capsule.

R. farragei A hairy shrub to about 1 m high; leaves are round to heart-shaped, green above and whitish beneath; flowers purplish with a dark centre. Occurs in areas subject to flooding on roadsides, creek beds.

Gossypium

There are about 30 species of this genus in tropical and sub-tropical parts of the world, with eight species in the northern and drier parts of Australia and three species occurring in the area. The commercial cotton plant belongs to this group. The genus consists of shrubs with small dark spots or oil glands; leaves are entire or lobed and the flowers differ from *Hibiscus* in the style being spirally twisted and not divided at the apex; there are only 3 lobes in the epicalyx and 3 to 5 chambers in the seed capsule.

G. sturtianum Sturt's Desert Rose. This plant is the Northern Territory floral emblem. An open shrub 1 to 2 m high, with smooth, spotted, egg-shaped to almost round leaves; flowers pink to lilac with a deep red centre, epicalyx lobes broad. Occurs on various rocky, sandy and gravelly soils, along watercourses, depressions and rocky gullies.

a   *Hibiscus sturtii*
b   Sturt's Desert Rose *Gossypium sturtianum*
c   *Gossypium australe*

G. australe A shrub 1 to 2 m high with closely hairy, narrow to broad, elliptical leaves with

a

c

b

less distinct spotting; flowers white to pink with a darker centre, epicalyx lobes very narrow. Occurs on sandy and gravelly soils, rocky hills.

Lavatera

This genus of trees, shrubs and herbs occurs in Western Europe, the Mediterranean, Central Asia and North America, with one species occurring in the area.

L. plebeia Native Hollyhock. An erect plant 1 to 3 m high, with 5 to 7 lobed leaves; flowers

white, pink or lilac, the column in the flower divided into a number of filaments, the style slender and the 5-lobed calyx twice as long as the 3 epicalyx lobes. Occurs on sandy soil, creek banks, areas subject to flooding and on roadsides.

Abutilon

This genus of herbs and shrubs is distributed throughout the warmer parts of the world with over 100 different species; ten species occur in the area. A number of selected exotic forms are cultivated as garden plants with common names such as Lantern Flowers, Chinese Lanterns, Indian Mallow. In China one of the species, *Abutilon avicennae*, is cultivated to provide Chinese jute. The Australian species have small, mostly yellow, saucer-shaped flowers; the end of the staminal column is divided into a number of filaments; the calyx has 5 lobes but there is no epicalyx; the fruit is a ring of papery seed cases, each with 3 or more seeds.

A. fraseri A small erect plant with heart- to egg-shaped, greyish green, woolly leaves; flowers yellow, single, on a long slender stalk. Common on rocky outcrops and rocky hillsides.

A. leucopetalum A small spreading plant, with greyish-green, round to egg/lance-shaped leaves with scalloped edges; flowers yellow, single. Occurs on rocky hillslopes and coarser type soils.

a   Native Hollyhock *Lavatera plebeia*
b   *Abutilon leucopetalum*
c   *Sida platycalyx*

Sida

The genus *Sida* is closely allied to *Abutilon*, but differs in having only one seed in each hard, honeycombed seed case. The flowers are yellow or orange, solitary or in terminal heads or spikes. There are over 200 species in the genus in the warmer parts of the world. Some species provide useful fibres and others have become weeds. There are a number of species in the area.

S. petrophila An erect shrub with greyish, woolly, oblong to linear/lance-shaped leaves, with scalloped edges. Flowers are yellow. Occurs on rocky soils and rocky hillsides.

S. cardiophylla A small erect shrub with dense greyish woolly hairs; leaves round, thick and woolly; flowers yellow. Occurs on red sand in association with *Spinifex*.

S. platycalyx Life-saver Burr. A prostrate to erect shrub with greyish, woolly round to heart-shaped, toothed leaves; flowers yellow. Occurs on various soils from heavy clays to red sands, often in disturbed soils.

Daisy Family   Asteraceae (Compositae)

In Central Australia following periods of rain, particularly in February and March, the arid areas literally come to life in late winter and spring, when the vast number of daisies, both annual and perennial, provide a kaleidoscope of colour, covering vast areas in yellow, white, pink, mauve, purple and blue.

The daisies belong to a very large family of plants widely distributed throughout the world. In Australia, as well as many different native species, there are numerous exotic types which have become naturalised, including many troublesome weeds such as various thistles, Bathurst Burr and dandelions. The family is botanically known as either Asteraceae or Compositae, the latter older name referring to the composite nature of the flower head.

The Nature of the Flower

With so many different daisies, it is often difficult to separate the various types, as only small features divide the various genera and species, so, to assist in understanding these characters, the following outline is given.

The Flowerhead

The so-called daisy flower consists of a number of small tubular flowers packed closely together into a head. These flowers may be either male, female or bisexual. The head may consist of all single flowers or small groups of flowers clustered together. The head of small flowers is surrounded at the base by a number of bracts which vary from green and leafy to soft, stiff, papery and petal-like. Collectively this group of bracts is known as an involucre. This surrounding involucre commonly forms a hemispherical or cylindrical shape, but sometimes may be spreading or even almost absent.

The Petals

In the typical daisy such as the exotic sunflower and gerbera, there is an outer ring of strap-like petals, which are soft and coloured and surround the yellow compressed centre of tiny flowers.

These strap-like petals arise from single flowers around the edge of the flowerhead, radiate outwards and are commonly called ray petals. There are various modifications to this outer petal arrangement, which may be small or even absent.

Papery Petal-like Bracts

In some groups of daisies, the outer radiating petals are replaced by a number of soft to stiff papery coloured bracts, forming the involucre. These bracts may radiate and give the appearance of petals, as in the paper daisies, e.g. *Helichrysum.* An interesting feature of the paper daisies is the manner in which these papery bracts quickly close around the flowerhead in the presence of moisture, slowly opening again as they become dry.

The Seed

The nature of the seed is frequently the separating character used to divide different genera and species. The seed is a small nut called an achne, which may be slender, cylindrical, flattened, rounded or egg-shaped, with a smooth, rough or hairy surface. Attached to the seed may be hairs, sharp scales, hooks or spines. Frequently at the top of the seed, there are a few to a number of bristles or scales forming a tuft, known as a pappus. A typical example of a pappus is the fluffy end on the seed of the dandelion and thistle. The nature of the pappus differs in the various species from sharp and spiny to soft and feathery and is an important character in separating the different species.

Understanding the Daisies

For convenience and to assist in understanding the different genera of daisies, they may be arranged into groups according to the presence or absence of petals. As there are large numbers of daisies, some of the more common genera are discussed.

Group 1 This group includes the typical daisy, usually with a yellow centre, surrounded by soft radiating, strap-like, coloured petals of white, yellow, pink, mauve, purple or blue. At the base of the flowerhead is a surrounding involucre of a number of herbaceous green to greyish green, or sometimes small papery bracts, forming a hemispherical to cylindrical surround. In this group are included genera such as *Senecio, Brachycome, Minuria, Calotis, Vittadinia, Podolepis, Olearia.*

Group 2 This group includes the paper daisies. The flowerheads do not have the outer ring of coloured, radiating, soft, straplike petals. There may be either numerous rows of soft to stiff papery bracts on the involucre or they may be close-fitting or almost absent. This group may be arranged into two smaller groups:

a) In this subgroup the papery bracts in colours of white, pink, yellow to yellowish brown, radiate around the central head of flowers in the manner of petals. An interesting feature of these paper daisies is the manner in which the papery bracts quickly close around the flowerhead in the presence of moisture, opening again when they become dry. Included in this group are the genera *Helichrysum, Helipterum, Waitzia, Myriocephalus, Cephalipterum.*

b) This subgroup usually has only a few papery bracts in the involucre and there are no radiating petal-like bracts, the flowerheads having a button-like appearance. Included in this group are *Craspedia, Calocephalus, Gnephosis, Angianthus, Pterocaulon; Rutidosis, Ixiolaena.*

Group 1

These typical daisies include both annual and perennial species; apart from some *Senecio* and *Podolepis,* most have flowerheads rarely exceeding 25 mm in diameter. The strap-like petals are in a range of various colours.

Senecio

There are nine species of *Senecio* in the area, three of which are widespread; all have bright yellow flowers with the green to greyish green involucral bracts arranged in a cylindrical manner. The seed heads are white and fluffy.

S. gregorii Yellow-Top. An annual to about 30 cm with fleshy, greyish green, narrow leaves and large single flowerheads at ends of stems. This species mainly occurs on sandplains and is common amongst mulga.

Yellow Top *Senecio gregorii*

S. magnificus Tall Yellow Top. A tall bushy perennial to about 1 m with thick fleshy, greyish green, broad, stem-clasping, toothed or entire leaves; the large flowerheads grow in clusters at ends of stems. This species commonly grows in sandy alluvial soils, floodways and edges of roadways.

S. lautus Variable Groundsel. A slender erect plant, 10 to 60 cm, with narrow dark green leaves; flowerheads in small clusters. Grows on various types of soils.

Podolepis

 a

There are four species of *Podolepis* in the area, all small annual plants with narrow leaves; the soft spreading petals are usually divided at the ends; the small papery involucral bracts are overlapping and form a somewhat conical-shaped base to the flowerhead; the seeds are slender and cylindrical.

P. jaceoides Showy Podolepis. An erect to spreading small plant with woolly soft leaves; the flowerheads have yellow petals and are carried on reddish brown stems. This species grows chiefly on red sandy soils.

P. capillaris A slender erect to spreading plant with narrow smooth leaves; flowerheads with white to cream petals on slender stalks. This species grows on sandy soils and stony slopes.

Brachycome

There are several different brachycomes in the area which are similar in appearance and require close examination of the seed to determine species. These soft, annual and perennial, spreading to erect plants are usually less than 30 cm in height and have divided or lobed small leaves; the flowerheads grow to about 25 mm with neatly arranged, soft, spreading petals of white, pink, mauve, lilac, purple or bluish tonings; the involucre of soft green bracts form a shallow, somewhat flattened hemisphere; the seeds are flat, short and about as long as the involucral bracts.

B. ciliaris Variable Daisy. As the common name suggests, this erect to spreading perennial has smooth to woolly, divided, or sometimes entire leaves; flower petals are white to purple. It is widely distributed on sandhills, gibbers, claypans and rock crevices.

B. iberidifolia Swan River Daisy. A small slender annual, 7 to 25 cm in height with smooth, divided leaves; flower petals white to violet; grows on sandplains, sandhills and water-courses.

Calotis

There are some eleven different *Calotis* species in the area. The flowers resemble those of *Brachycome* except that a number have yellow petals; leaves are not basal and are

 d

usually entire, toothed or lobed; the seed heads have small sharp scales, awns or spines attached to the seed forming prickly burrs. These burrs can be most uncomfortable to the traveller, for example, *Calotis hispidula* (Hairy Burr-daisy or Bogan Flea) has several hairy scales with sharp awns which work into the clothing, bringing about itching of the skin.

C. hispidula Hairy Burr-daisy, Bogan Flea. A prostrate to spreading annual, 5 to 15 cm high; leaves narrow, wedge- to somewhat lance-shaped; flowerheads with very small yellow petals, involucre shallow, rough; seeds with 5 to 6 stiff spreading awns and short hairy scales. Occurs on a wide range of soils.

a Tall Yellow Top *Senecio magnificus*
b Variable Groundsel *Senecio lautus*
c Swan River Daisy *Brachycome iberidifolia*
d Showy Podolepis *Podolepis jaceoides*
e Blue-burr Daisy *Calotis cuneifolia*

C. cuneifolia Blue-burr Daisy. An erect to spreading plant 30 cm or more in height with small spoon-shaped, lobed leaves; the flower petals are white to blue. This species grows on sandy soils and clayey loams.

C. latiuscula Yellow-Burr Daisy. An erect plant 9 to 40 cm in height with oblong to wedge-shaped, coarsely-toothed leaves; the flower petals are yellow; occurs on sandy, loamy and rocky soils.

Minuria

This group of daisies with seven species in the area has *Brachycome*-like flowers and consists of low, erect to spreading, annual or perennial plants with entire or coarsely-toothed leaves; the flowerheads have a number of fine spreading petals of white to purplish hue; the involucre is usually bell-shaped; the slender flattened seeds have several white fine bristly projections from the top.

M. leptophylla Minnie Daisy. A spreading bushy cushion-forming plant, 10 to 30 cm high, with narrow leaves. The numerous flowerheads have white to purplish petals and are produced in profusion, almost obscuring the leaves. This species grows chiefly on sandy and stony type soils.

M. denticulata Woolly Minuria. An erect, slender to much branched, woolly plant, 10 to 30 cm in height, with narrow, entire or toothed leaves; flower petals white to blue, closely arranged. This species favours sandplains, dunes, gibbers and areas subject to flooding for short periods.

Vittadinia

This group of small perennial plants have flower heads resembling *Brachycome,* but with narrower petals; the green bracts at the base of the flowerhead form a bell-shaped to cylindrical involucre. The narrow seed has several long spreading bristles, and a number of seeds collectively form a tufted head.

V. triloba Fuzzweed. A small spreading plant 10 to 30 cm high with entire or lobed small woolly leaves; flowerheads have white, mauve to purple petals; occurs on various types of soils.

Olearia

There are about five different species in the area, which consist of perennial, woolly to sticky, bushy shrubs from 30 cm to 1.5 m in height; the leaves are woolly or sticky, entire, toothed or lobed; the flowerheads with white, pink to bluish petals are commonly produced in clusters; the involucre of green bracts with rough edges is usually arranged in a cylindrical manner; the seeds are cylindrical with a number of bristles arising from the top.

O. stuartii An erect hairy shrub 30 to 60 cm high with the usually toothed leaves tapered to the base; the flower petals are pink to blue. This species occurs on red sandy soil and on rocky slopes.

O. subspicata Spiked Daisy Bush. A bushy erect shrub to 1.5 m high with greyish white new growth; flowers with only a few white spreading petals. This species prefers deep red sandy soils.

Group 2a

Helichrysum

This group of paper daisies includes both annual herbs and shrubs with an involucre of numerous yellow, white or pink, stiff, papery bracts, which radiate in the manner of petals. Some species have small flowerheads with close-fitting, thin bracts, with a number of heads with short stalks forming a small to large head of flowers. The seed is usually cylindrical to egg-shaped; there is a pappus of fine bristles which is feathery at the apex.

a Minnie Daisy *Minuria leptophylla*
b Spiked Daisy Bush *Olearia subspicata*
c Yellow Everlasting *Helichrysum bracteatum*
d Helichrysum, Senecio, Erodium
e Pink Everlasting *Helichrysum cassinianum*
f Helichrysum apiculatum

There are about ten different species in the area.

H. bracteatum Yellow Everlasting. An erect perennial 20 to 60 cm in height with smooth to woolly stems and leaves which are soft, stem-clasping, lance-shaped, narrow to egg-shaped; flowerheads yellow, up to 50 mm wide, occurring single at the end of a long flower stem with numerous shiny yellow straw-like bracts radiating in a petal-like manner; occurs on a range of soils, particularly around edges of clay-pans and drainage areas.

H. cassinianum Pink Everlasting. A small erect annual, 9 to 60 cm high, with narrow, greyish green, chiefly basal leaves; the flowerheads, 15 to 20 mm wide, have soft, white to pink, papery, spreading, petal-like bracts, with a number of heads in a cluster at the top of stems. It occurs on sandplains, frequently growing amongst mulga.

H. davenportii Pink Everlasting. An erect annual with narrow lance-shaped leaves, forming a rosette at ground level; the flowerheads, 25 to 50 mm wide, occur singly on a long flower stalk; the involucre is hemispherical, with a single row of white to pink papery petal-like bracts radiating beyond the yellow centre. This species occurs in sandy soil amongst mulga and spinifex.

H. apiculatum An erect to spreading, variable plant, with a number of slender woolly stems; narrow, lance-shaped to egg-shaped, greyish, woolly leaves; small golden heads, 6 to 10 mm in diameter, with a number of heads at the ends of stems; the heads have numerous small, closely arranged, papery bracts which are barely spreading; occurs on various types of soils.

a   *Helipterum* species
b   White Paper Daisy *Helipterum floribundum*
c   *Cephalipterum drummondii*
d   Poached-egg Daisy *Myriocephalus stuartii*

Helipterum

This genus closely resembles *Helichrysum*, but generally the papery bracts are softer, the seed is often angular and the pappus of five bristles is feathery from the base to the apex. There are about eighteen different species in the area.

H. floribundum White Paper Daisy. A small branched, woolly, spreading to erect annual, 4 to 40 cm in height, with narrow, woolly leaves chiefly at the base; the flowerheads, 10 to 20 mm wide, have numerous, soft, white, spreading, papery, petal-like bracts, forming a hemispherical involucre. As with other paper daisies, the bracts quickly close around the yellow flowerheads when moisture is present, giving the impression that flowers are still in the bud stage; common on sandplains and amongst mulga.

H. stipitatum Yellow Everlasting. An erect to spreading, greyish, hairy plant, 40 to 60 cm in height, with linear to lance-shaped leaves; the single flowerheads, 14 to 30 cm across with a hemisperical involucre, have numerous yellow, short, closely arranged, spreading, soft, papery bracts; occurs on sandy soils often amongst spinifex.

H. moschatum Musk Sunray. This erect woolly plant with narrow, lance-shaped, greyish, white leaves, has clusters of small heads of pale yellow flowers with close-fitting, thin, papery bracts; occurring on sandy soils.

Waitzia

This genus resembles *Helichrysum* and *Helipterum*, but bracts are more numerous, narrow and in many rows; the seeds are tapered to the apex and the pappus of fine bristles is not feathery, but has fine barbs. There are two species in the area.

W. acuminata Orange Immortal. An erect annual, 5 to 60 cm in height, with narrow, stem-clasping leaves; the bell-shaped flowerheads, 7 to 10 mm broad, have numerous narrow rows of lance-shaped, soft, yellow to orange, petal-like bracts; flowers often have the appearance of being closed; occurs on sandplains, dunes and stony outcrops.

W. citrinus Is similar to *W. acuminata*, but is smaller and heads are hemispherical.

Cephalipterum

There is only one species in this genus, *C. drummondii*. This paper daisy has a number of separate small flower heads, each with small, spreading, yellow to pink, papery bracts grouped together forming the globular head; the seed is egg-shaped, woolly with a scale at the apex. This slender erect annual, 5 to 30 cm high, has narrow leaves and yellow to pink flowerheads; grows on sandy soils in the north-west of South Australia.

Myriocephalus

This daisy differs from the other paper daisies with radiating papery bracts, in that the yellow centre of the flower consists of groups of small heads with thin, close-fitting, papery involucres forming a large compound head, surrounded by a general involucre of numerous white to greenish, narrow, petal-like bracts in many rows. The seed is cylindrical with a pappus of one to a number of bristles. There are three species in the area.

M. stuartii Poached Egg Daisy. An erect, woolly annual, 10 to 50 cm high, with narrow to lance-shaped, woolly leaves; the heads are 2 to 4 cm across with numerous, white, papery, petal-like bracts. Common on sandplains and dunes.

M. rhizocephalus This unusual daisy has prostrate stems and long, grass-like leaves; the flower heads, which grow amongst the leaves, have a yellow centre with greenish white bracts. Occurs on various soil types which are moist.

Group 2b

This group of daisies have button-like heads of yellow flowers without petals or spreading involucral bracts.

Craspedia

This genus has numerous small heads of 3 to 10 tiny flowers with a close-fitting involucre of thin bracts, clustered tightly together into a globular, oblong to egg-shaped, dense, yellow, compact head; there are tiny bracts between the small groups of flowers which are not apparent unless the flower is dissected. The generally small bracts of the compound head are concealed by the individual flowers. The small seed is egg-shaped, silky, hairy and the pappus has 9 to 20 feathery bristles. There are three species in the area.

C. pleiocephala Billy Buttons. An erect annual with slightly woolly stems 5 to 30 cm in height, with green, lance- to egg-shaped, slightly hairy leaves; flower heads yellow, about 1 cm across, with small involucral bracts. Occurs on various types of soil.

C. chrysantha Billy Buttons. An erect annual with grey woolly stems and narrow leaves, 6 to 25 cm high; flowerheads yellow, oval to oblong, about 1 cm diameter. Occurs on various types of soil.

Calocephalus

This genus resembles *Craspedia,* however there are no tiny bracts between the groups of flowers and the heads are globular; the seeds are without silky hairs and the pappus has several flattened bristles joined at the base.

C. platycephalus A small woolly plant, 8 to 45 cm in height, with narrow grey woolly leaves; flower heads globular, 1 to 2 cm across. Occurs on sandy soil.

Gnephosis

This genus resembles *Craspedia* with globular yellow flowerheads which have a few leaf-like bracts at the base. The seeds are compressed, narrowed to the base, either smooth or hairy; the pappus may be absent, cup-like or of small bristles. There are four species in the area.

G. foliata An erect annual, 5 to 30 cm in height, with narrow woolly leaves; flowerheads are globular, depressed and about 1 cm in diameter. Occurs on saline-type soils.

Angianthus

This genus differs from *Craspedia* in the club-shaped, cylindrical to egg-shaped flower heads, with a few leaf-like bracts at the base of the head. The seeds are egg-shaped with a rough surface; the pappus is variable, absent or with one or more jagged scales, sometimes crown-like. There are three species in the area.

A. tomentosa Hairy Cup Flower. A woolly annual with erect stems, 5 to 30 cm high, with narrow, elliptical, woolly leaves. The yellow heads are at first egg-shaped, becoming cylindrical as they develop. Occurs on a wide range of soils and habitats.

Pterocaulon

This genus which extends into Asia and America differs from the above four genera. The dense compound globular heads are pinkish, with the ends of the smaller flowerheads projecting in a pincushion-like manner. There is no general involucre except for a few floral leaves at the base of the head.

a Billy Buttons *Craspedia chrysantha*
b *Calocephalus platycephalus*
c Apple Bush *Pterocaulon sphacelatum*
d Grey Wrinklewort *Rutidosis helichrysoides*

The seeds are cylindrical, slightly flattened and slightly hairy with a pappus of slender bristles. There are two species in the area which look somewhat alike, *P. sphacelatum* and *P. serrulatum.*

P. sphacelatum Apple Bush. A stiff erect plant 30 to 60 cm high, woolly to rough across the foliage, with a fruity odour when crushed; the narrow, rough leaves are oblong in shape; the globular to egg-shaped heads, 8 to 20 mm in diameter, are pinkish. Occurs on sandy and clayey loams, flooded areas and gibber plains.

Rutidosis

This genus has simple yellow flowerheads at the end of a long slender stem; these are formed from a number of small single flowers which project slightly; the head, which is hemispherical, becomes more globular as the flowers develop. The involucre is hemispherical with a number of short stiff overlapping bracts; the outer flowers overhang the involucral bracts. The seed is oblong to conical with a rough surface and a pappus of narrow fringed scales. There is one species in the area.

R. helichrysoides Grey Wrinklewort. An erect variable woolly plant, 25 to 60 cm high, with long narrow woolly leaves; flowerheads bright yellow up to 1 cm across with several heads at the ends of branches. Occurs on sandy and loamy soils, often near water.

Ixiolaena

This genus is somewhat like *Rutidosis,* but the involucre is bell-shaped to cylindrical with rough green involucral bracts. Seed are cylindrical, slightly compressed, surface is hairy; the pappus has finely barbed bristles.

I. tomentosa Woolly Plover Daisy. A much-branched, rough to woolly plant, 20 to 40 cm in height; leaves lance-shaped with a pointed apex; heads yellow, bell-shaped. Occurs chiefly on heavy soils.

Geranium Family   Geraniaceae

Although there are a number of geraniums in Australia, mostly with very small flowers, they do not occur in Central Australia. However, a related genus, *Erodium*, is common in the drier parts of the continent.

Erodium

This genus with about 60 species is widely distributed around the Mediterranean. In addition to the native species in the central Australian area, there are also three exotic naturalised species. These annual or short-lived, low-growing herbs have lobed or deeply dissected leaves; the small flowers with 5 blue to purplish or pink or white petals are followed by fruit with an extended beak with 5 seeds; the beak splits into spirally coiled awns, to each of which a seed is attached. The different species look much alike.

E. cygnorum Crowfoot. A spreading herb with slender, finely hairy stems; leaves with 3 principal lobes; flowers blue with purplish to reddish or white to yellowish veins towards base of petals; fruit with a long beak. Occurs on sandy soils, commonly in association with daisies and pea flowers.

E. crinitum Native Crowfoot. Similar to *E. cygnorum*, but leaves more deeply lobed, stems hairier; flowers blue with white marking towards the base of petals. Occurs on sandy soil.

a Native Crowsfoot *Erodium crinitum*
b Round-leaved Parakeela *Calandrinia remota*
c Broad-leaved Parakeela *Calandrinia balonen.*

Portulaca Family   Portulacaceae

This family is better known by the cultivated garden forms of the exotic *Portulaca grandiflora* from Argentina. The family consists of succulent plants, with four genera in the area, most of which have small, usually yellow, flowers. One genus, *Calandrinia*, has several species with large attractive flowers.

Calandrinia Parakeela

This group of succulent spreading plants have fleshy taproots and fleshy succulent leaves and stems. The leaves are grouped at the base of the plant. There are 5, or sometimes more, soft shiny spreading, pink purple or white petals, with a few to a number of stamens. Many of the species are similar in appearance and several species with larger flowers are discussed.

C. balonensis Broad Leaved Parakeela. A fleshy, clump-forming plant, with broad lance-shaped leaves, concave on the upper surface; flowers are large, purplish, with several flowers on a long stalk. Occurs on red sandy loam, sand plains and dunes, often amongst mulga.

C. polyandra Parakeela. A plant similar to *C. balonensis*, but leaves are narrower, flattened and grooved on the upper surface. Occurs in similar locations to *C. balonensis*. Some authorities regard *C. remota* as *C. polyandra* and vice versa.

C. remota Round Leaved Parakeela. A plant with a similar growth to *C. balonensis*, but leaves are cylindrical and flowers are frequently on longer stems. Occurs in similar locations to *C. balonensis*.

Amaranth Family   Amaranthaceae

This family is distributed throughout the warmer parts of the world and a number of the exotic species are cultivated as garden plants such as Tassel Flowers *Amaranthus,* Globe or Bachelor Buttons *Gomphrena,* Cockscomb *Celosia.* There are ten genera in Australia, the most showy group being *Ptilotus.* An unusual genus with one species in the area is *Achyranthes.*

Ptilotus

This large widespread genus has a number of different species which are given common names such as Mulla Mulla, Pussy Tails, Feather Tails and the like. The genus consists of annuals and perennials which may be spreading to erect herbs and undershrubs, with alternate leaves; the flowers have long fluffy stamens, with a large number arranged into globular to cylindrical, fluffy bottlebrush-like heads, which may be small or large and vary in colour from cream to green or pink. A number of species are widespread in the area.

P. exaltatus Pink Mulla Mulla. A robust plant which may grow to 1 m high, with soft smooth leaves of various shapes, crowded at the base of the plant and on stems; flowerheads pink, conical to cylindrical, 3 to 15 cm long and to 4 cm diameter. Occurs on a wide range of soils, sand ridges, mulga woodland, rocky outcrops.

P. helipteroides Hairy Mulla Mulla. A small plant with silky lance-shaped leaves; flowerheads cylindrical to somewhat globular. Occurs on sandy and gravelly flats and hillsides.

P. macrocephalus Large Green Pussytail, Feather Head. An annual or perennial plant

with a woody taproot and long stems; leaves dark green, linear to narrow lance-shaped; flowerheads variable, hemispherical to cylindrical, pale green, fragrant. occurs in a wide range of locations on red sandy loam, heavy moist clayey soils, on low rocky rises.

P. obovatus Silver Bush, Silver Tails, White Foxtail. A bushy plant with several varieties, from 10 cm to 1 m high, with woolly, silvery, egg-shaped to elliptical/lance-shaped leaves; flowerheads pale pink, globular and numerous. Occurs on various soils and locations.

P. polystachyus Long Tails, Bottle Washers, Prince of Wales Feathers. A clump forming plant with slender, erect to spreading stems; leaves linear to lance-shaped; flowerheads long, slender, cylindrical, often bent, yellowish green to red. Occurs on a wide range of habitats, alluvial flats, gravelly and stony areas, dunes and along roadsides.

Achyranthes

This genus occurs in warmer parts of the world with about 100 species. In the area there is one species which also extends beyond Australia.

A. aspera An erect plant with numerous branches; leaves soft and egg-shaped; flowers small, pink, in long slender spikes. Occurs chiefly in rocky gullies.

a Pink Mulla Mulla *Ptilotus exaltatus*
b Hairy Mulla Mulla *Ptilotus helipteroides*
c Large Green Pussytail *Ptilotus macrocephalus*
d *Ptilotus macrocephalus*
e Long Tails *Ptilotus polystachyus*
f Silver Bush *Ptilotus obovatus*
g *Achyranthes aspera*

Cabbage Family   Cruciferae

This large family of plants is widespread in the northern hemisphere, with a number of different genera in the area, including introduced weeds such as Wild Mustard and Wild Turnip which are widely distributed. Within the family there are important vegetables such as cabbage, cauliflower, broccoli, mustard and many others; there are also a number of garden flowers, such as stocks *(Malcolmia)* and *Alyssum*. One of the genera, *Blennodia,* is widely distributed and may cover wide areas after rains.

Blennodia

A group of annuals with two species in Australia which also occur in the area. These are small plants with leaves at the base and a number of slender stems which arise from ground level; the small 4-petalled flowers are followed by cylindrical seed pods with numerous seed.

B . canescens Wild Stock. A small annual with slender lobed leaves; flowers white, pink or lavender, in slender sprays. Occurs on sandy loams, stony soils, or on dunes.

a   Wild Stock *Blennodia canescens*
b   *Blennodia canescens*
c   Early Nancy *Anguillaria centralis*
d   Grass Tree *Xanthorrhoea thorntonii*

Lily and Amaryllid Families Liliaceae, Amaryllidaceae

Australia has a number of members of the lily family, which is better known by the exotic *Lilium* with its large trumpet-shaped flowers. The Australian members have mainly small flowers and are generally inconspicuous, unless a number are present. One of the genera *Xanthorrhoea*, Grass Tree, has literally thousands of tiny flowers on a large spike.

The Amaryllid family, which has about 1000 species in warmer parts of the world, is represented in Australia by twenty species, only one of which occurs in the area.

Lilies Liliaceae

Anguillaria
(regarded as *Wurmbea* by some)

Formerly regarded as having only one species, *A. dioica,* in the area, this has been now divided into three species, all much alike.

A. dioica Early Nancy. A small bulbous herb with 1 to several narrow fleshy leaves; the small, 6-petalled flowers, white to pink with 6 stamens, occur singly or in short sprays. Occurs in moist sandy loam.

A. centralis Early Nancy. A small bulbous plant with soft linear to lance-shaped leaves; flowers deep pink, with a number on a slender spike. Occurs in sandy loam, only in the Olgas.

Xanthorrhoea
Xanthorrhoeaceae

Commonly known as Grass Trees or Black Boys, there are about fifteen different species in Australia, one of which occurs in the area.

X. thorntonii Grass Tree, Black Boy. A robust plant with a stout trunk to about 20 cm diameter and up to 3 m high; leaves numerous, long, angular and sharply pointed and

crowded in a dense head; flowers tiny, white, with 6 petals, crowded in a stout dense spike to about 2 m long; flowers followed by sharp black seed capsules. Occurs on sandplains.

Amaryllids
Amaryllidaceae

Crinum

There are about ten species of *Crinum* in Australia, with one species found in the area.

These herbaceous plants with a bulbous root have fleshy leaves and white to cream flowers with 6 petals (perianth segment) and 6 stamens. The species from dry areas have contractile roots which shrivel during dry periods, pulling the bulbous root deeper into the soil; in old plants the bulb may be 60 cm or more below ground level.

C. flaccidum Darling or Murray Lily. A bulbous plant with fleshy strap-like leaves to about 60 cm long which die down during dry periods; flowers cream to yellowish about 5 cm wide with several flowers on a long fleshy stalk. Occurs in moist areas such as flood plains, appearing in large numbers after rain.

a

Potato Family Solanaceae

This large family of plants is widely distributed throughout the world, particularly in Central and South America. There are many important food plants included, such as the potato (*Solanum tuberosum*), the tomato (*Lycopersicon lycopersicum*) and many others, as well as many ornamental plants such as petunia and browallia. Some of the plants are poisonous and others are used to obtain medical drugs. The family is well represented in Australia with a number of introduced naturalised species. Amongst the genera seen in the area are *Solanum, Nicotinia, Datura, Duboisia*.

b

c

d

a   Darling Lily *Crinum flaccidum*
b   Wild Tomato *Solanum quadriloculatum*
c   Potato Bush *Solanum ellipticum*
d   *Nicotinia occidentalis*

S. ellipticum Potato Bush, Wild Gooseberry. A spreading greyish perennial, with close short dense hairs on all parts, with a few to a number of prickles on stems, flower stalks and sometimes on leaves; leaves greyish, elliptical to egg-shaped, often with wavy edges and purplish towards base; flowers purple with close yellow stamens; fruit globular, yellowish green, often tinged with purple. A widespread species, common on sandy and stony soils. Fruit eaten by Aborigines.

Solanum

This large genus is widely distributed throughout the world as well as Australia, with some twenty different native species in the area and one naturalised species, *S. nigrum*, Black Nightshade. The genus consists of perennial and annual herbs and shrubs, commonly with prickles on the stems, leaves and flower calyx. The fleshy, often felty, leaves are entire, coarsely toothed or lobed; flowers are in shades of purple and blue, with the lower part of the flower a short tube, with 4 to 5 spreading lobes at the apex and 5 yellow distinct stamens; the fruit is like a small tomato, yellowish to greenish purple or reddish in colour. The fruit of some species is eaten by Aborigines. Many of the species look very similar and require close examination to separate. Two of the more widespread species are discussed.

S. quadriloculatum Wild Tomato. An erect to spreading, greyish green plant with numerous prickles on stems, leaves, flower stalks and calyx; the leaves are elliptical with entire edges; flowers are purple, usually with a number in a spray; the yellowish green fruit is globular. A widespread species, occurring on sandy and gravelly soils, on plains and banks of watercourses.

Nicotinia

This genus is chiefly found in North and South America, with commercial tobacco being produced from two of the species. There are about ten different species in the area and several varieties. This group of annuals to short-lived perennials generally has the leaves grouped together at ground level, with smaller leaves on the flowering stems; the flowers are white to yellow, sometimes tinged with purple, trumpet-shaped with a slender tube and 5 lobes at the apex, and grow in groups at the ends of stems. The flowers close in full sunlight and open in the shade or after sunset. The fruit is a smooth capsule.

N. occidentalis A small erect plant to about 0.5 m in height; leaves clustered at base of plant, elliptical to lance-shaped, with small leaves on the flower stalk; flowers white. Occurs often in part shaded areas in sandy, stony to heavy soils.

N. excelsior An erect large growing plant to 1 m or more in height with elliptical to lance-shaped leaves; flowers white to yellowish with a long corolla tube. Occurs in gullies and along creek banks.

a

b

c

Datura

There is only one Australian species in the area and two exotic naturalised species. The genus consists of strong growing annuals or plants which die back to a perennial root base; the flowers are funnel-shaped, longer than those in *Nicotinia* and occur singly in the forks of the branches. The fruit is a capsule, but differs from *Nicotinia* in being covered with sharp spines.

D. leichhardtia Thorn Apple. An erect growing plant to 1 m or more in height; the leaves are egg-shaped to rhomboidal with wavy or coarsely toothed margins; the flowers are white or sometimes tinged with red, the tube is 4 to 7 cm in length and there are 5 spreading lobes; the fruit is globular with numerous slender spines. Occurs on a variety of soils, along watercourses and on plains areas.

Duboisia

There are three species of *Duboisia* in Australia, two of which occur in rainforests of the east coast. An important medical drug is obtained from the leaves of the rainforest species. These shrubs to small trees have corky bark; the leaves are alternate and the flowers are bell-shaped with 5 turned back lobes; the fruit is a fleshy berry.

D. hopwoodii Pituri. An erect, smooth, bushy shrub with linear to elliptical leaves; the white flowers have a short, broad, tubular section and 5 spreading lobes with purple striping on the throat of the flower; there are 4 stamens, 2 of which are shorter than the others; the small globular fruit is black. Occurs mainly on red sandy ridges. The dried leaves, after preparation, are chewed by Aborigines.

Borage Family   Boraginaceae

This large family of plants is widely distributed in temperate and tropical parts of the world and consists of shrubs and herbs with hairy foliage and tubular, 5-lobed flowers. The family includes a number of plants valued by beekeepers for the production of honey, cultivated garden plants such as forget-me-not (*Myosotis*), heliotrope (*Heliotropus*) and many others and numerous introduced weeds such as Paterson's Curse or Salvation Jane (*Echium lycopis*). Of the species in the area two of the genera have very shiny flowers.

Trichodesma

This genus extends to Africa and Asia with one species occurring in the area, a herb with soft, hairy, alternate or opposite leaves; flowers with a short tube, 5 spreading lobes and the stamens closely arranged around the pistil in a twisted, column-like beak; the calyx is deeply 5-lobed.

T. zeylanicum Cattlebush. A slender plant 60 cm to 1 m high, with soft hairy narrow to broad lance-shaped leaves; flowers light blue, white or sometimes reddish. Occurs on sand dunes, red sandy loam and on rocky hills.

Halgania

This genus is confined to Australia with about fifteen species, with several species occurring in the area. The genus is closely allied to *Trichodesma*, but consists of shrubs with alternate leaves, deep blue flowers with the columns not twisted and the fruit separated into 4 one-seeded cases, whereas in *Trichodesma* the fruit splits into 2 two-sided cases.

H. glabra A small sticky shrub to about 50 cm high with lance-shaped to oblong entire or toothed leaves; flowers deep blue in loose sprays. Occurs on rocky hills and in gullies.

a Pituri *Duboisia hopwoodii*
b Cattle Bush *Trichodesma zeylanicum*
c *Hibbertia glaberrima*

Hibbertia Family   Dilleniaceae

There are over 100 different *Hibbertia* species, most of which occur in south western Western Australia and eastern Australia; there is one species in the area.

H. glaberrima A bushy shrub 1 to 2 m high with short, smooth, dark green, oblong to elliptical leaves; flowers 2 to 3 cm diameter, bright yellow, with 5 petals and numerous stamens. Occurs in protected rocky gullies and hillsides.

Cassia Family   Caesalpiniaceae

There are three groups or genera in this family, *Cassia*, *Petalostylis* and *Lysiphyllum* (formerly included with *Bauhinia*). The plants are mostly shrubs, some tall, except for *Lysiphyllum* which grow into small trees. The family is widely distributed throughout the area and grows in a wide variety of soil types.

Cassia

There are a number of different kinds of cassia from small to large, slender or bushy shrubs. The leaves of green to silvery grey are mostly leather type, with a few to a number of leaflets; some have a single leaf (called a phyllode). The bright yellow flowers grow in clusters and have 5 petals arranged in a saucer-shaped fashion with 10 stamens which become darker in colour. There is a slender curved style towards one side of the flower. The cassias are widely distributed and may dominate an area, particularly in sandy type soils.

Examples of some of the more common types are discussed.

C. artemisioides Silver Cassia. This bushy shrub grows from 1 to 2 m high and is one of the most showy of all the cassias in the area. The silvery grey leaves, with a few to a number of narrow leaflets, contrast attractively against other vegetation. The flowers are sweetly scented. This cassia occurs in various soils but prefers sandy and rocky types.

C. nemophila (syn. *C. eremophila*). This widely distributed cassia grows in various soils but is more common on sandy types. A slender to bushy shrub, growing from 1 to 3 m high, it has green to greyish green, slightly hairy leaves, with one to two pairs of leaflets. The flowers are arranged in groups of 3 to 10 and the petals are unequal. There are four different varieties of this *Cassia* which differ chiefly in the leaflet arrangement.

Variety *nemophila* In this variety there are 2 pairs of narrow leaflets which may be cylindrical and hooked or flattened. In older leaves the leaflets may be shed, leaving the stalks which give the appearance of narrow single leaves.

Variety *coriacea* In this variety the leaves are short with 2 to 8 pairs of leaflets which are variable and may be elliptical, egg-shaped or broad and shallowly channelled.

Variety *platypoda* The leaves of this variety are unusual with a flattened leaf stalk (phyllode) which may be narrow, lance-shaped, or broad to wedge-shaped, with 2 small flattened to cylindrical leaflets at the end; frequently these leaflets fall off at an early stage.

Variety *zygophylla* The leaves of this variety are longer and have 1 to 2 pairs of leaflets, which are narrow, elliptical to egg-shaped.

C. sturtii This widely distributed variable species grows in different soil types and is a bushy shrub 1 to 2 m high. The whitish grey, hairy or sometimes smooth foliage has leaves with 3 to 6 pairs of leaflets, varying from broad and linear to egg-shaped; there are 4 to 5 flowers grouped together.

C. pleurocarpa Stripe Pod Cassia, Fire Bush. This cassia, occurring on sandy soils and sand dunes, grows as an erect shrub, sometimes suckering freely and forming closely arranged groups of plants. The leaves have 5 to 9 pairs of narrow, oblong, thick, yellowish green leaflets. The flowers grow in long sprays and the petals are unequal. The flat seed pods have a raised line along each side and black stripes across the pod.

C. helmsii This bushy shrub, often rounded or flat-topped, is silvery grey and grows in sandy and rocky soils. The leaves have 3 to 4 pairs of broad, somewhat angular leaflets with the narrow ends towards the leaf stalk. There are 4 to 10 flowers with oval petals which grow in short spreading heads.

C. notabilis Cockroach Bush. A small short-lived shrub to about 0.5 to 1 m in height; leaves with a number of lance-shaped hairy leaflets; a number of flowers are produced on a slender flower stem. The seed pods are attractive, particularly when a number are produced, being 2 to 3 cm long and a centimetre or more wide, with raised blackish brown markings across the seed case, resembling the body of a cockroach. This species is more common in the northern parts of the area and grows on gravelly and sandy soils.

C. venusta A spreading shrub 1 to 2 m high; leaves with 6 to 15 pairs of greenish-grey leaflets with pointed apex; flowers yellow with a number on a long flower-stalk. Occurs on sandy and rocky soils.

C. phyllodinea Silver Cassia. A spreading shrub 0.5 to 2 m in height, with silvery grey stems and leaves. Unlike the other cassias, the leaves are not divided; the leaf stalk is flattened into a phyllode as in most acacias and is narrow to lance-shaped or oblong in shape, but in young plants the leaf stalk may have 2 small leaflets; there are 2 to 5 flowers on a short flower stalk. This species occurs on both rocky and sandy soils.

a   Silver Cassia *Cassia artemisioides*
b   *Cassia nemophila* var. *platypoda*
c   *Cassia pleurocarpa*
d   *Cassia helmsii*
e   *Cassia venusta*

Petalostylis

There are two different species in this genus which is closely allied to *Cassia* but differs in the feathery leaves having a single leaflet at the end; the flowers have 5 stamens of which 3 only are fertile; the curved style is flattened and petal-like; one of the petals is usually marked with red at the base.

P. cassioides This spreading shrub to 1.5 m high has long leaves, with 23 to 55 small egg-shaped to wedge-shaped leaflets; the yellow flowers have a red patch at the base of one petal. This plant favours rocky and sandy soils and occurs throughout the area.

a

P. labicheoides An erect shrub to 2 m high. It differs from *P. cassioides,* having only 5 to 15 leaflets which are longer and lance-shaped. Occurring in rocky and sandy soils, this species does not occur in the Northern Territory.

Lysiphyllum

(formerly included with *Bauhinia*)

There is only one species in the area, *L. gilvum* (syn. *L. cunninghamii*). This large bushy shrub to small spreading tree to 9 m high has leaves with a pair of egg-shaped leaflets. The red pea flowers have small petals and projecting stamens. The flowers are followed by oblong, slightly curved seed pods. This plant grows chiefly in plains areas on various soil types.

Pea Family Fabaceae

The Pea Family is a member of a large group of plants to which the acacia and cassia also belong. This group of plants has the common characteristic of the seeds being contained in a pod known as a legume. The pea flowers are characterised by having flowers shaped like the exotic Sweet Pea. In this form of flower there are 5 petals; the two lower or middle ones are joined and folded downwards forming a ridge called a keel, the two side petals may be spreading or close against the keel and are known as wings and the upper petal is often upstanding and showy and is known as a standard. The size of the flower and petals vary in different species, for example: in Sturt's Desert Pea, the standard is large, showy and folded backwards, the keel is long and pointed and the two wings are small and folded close against the keel; in contrast, flowers of the twining *Glycine* are small and the petals are all of a similar size. The stamens number 10, but, unlike many flowers, they are not usually visible, being covered by the folded petals of the keel. The seed pods differ in shape and contain from one to numerous seeds. Many of the pea flowers of Central Australia are annuals but there are a number of perennial types. The plants vary from small herbaceous types to small trees and grow in a wide variety of soil types but particularly in sandy and rocky soils.

As there are a large number of different pea flowers, some of the more widespread and obvious types are discussed.

Clianthus

There is only one species of this genus in Australia, *Clianthus formosus,* Sturt's Desert Pea; the only other species, *Clianthus puniceus,* occurs in New Zealand. This plant is the most spectacular of all the pea flowers; it is an annual spreading plant, which may form large clumps. The soft grey feather leaves have

a number of silvery grey woolly leaflets; the large, shiny, brilliant red flowers usually have a dark purplish-black patch on the turned back standard. Sometimes the flowers may be white. This plant grows on a variety of soils but particularly sandy loams.

a   *Petalostylis cassioides*
b   *Lysiphyllum gilvum*
c   Sturt's Desert Pea *Clianthus formosus*

Psoralea

This group of plants is better known by the commonly cultivated, large, bushy, exotic garden shrub, *Psoralea pinnata*. The Australian species, of which there are eight different kinds in Central Australia, are slender to erect or spreading plants, mostly with 3 leaflets, and with numerous small flowers in slender spikes. Although some grow on sand plains and dunes, most occur on flood plains and rocky hillslopes. Two of the more common and more apparent species are discussed.

P. australasica (formerly included with *P. patens*). An erect growing plant to about 1 m in height, with greyish green leaves and 3 egg-shaped to rhomboid, or broad lance-shaped, finely-toothed leaflets. The small pink to bluish pea flowers are crowded on a long slender stem. This species occurs along waterways and flood plains.

P. cinerea This plant is similar to *Psoralea patens*, but the leaflets are elliptical to egg-shaped with a short point at the apex. The pink to purple flowers grow in groups of 3 on a long crowded flower stem. This species usually grows on flood plains and other areas subject to flooding.

Erythrina

There are some 200 different species of *Erythrina* throughout the world, with four Australian species, found in the northern parts of the continent. One species, *Erythrina vespertilio*, known as Bean Tree or Batwing Coral Tree, extends southwards to north eastern South Australia. The Bean Tree is a spreading tree, 5 to 12 m in height, with rough corky bark and prickly branches. The leaves are divided into 2 curved batwing-like lobes and, during dry periods, may become deciduous. The red flowers have a long standard, a small keel and wings with the stamens projecting; the flat broad seed pods have shiny red seeds. This small tree grows on ridges, watercourses and some floodplains.

Swainsona

There are a number of different kinds of *Swainsona*, many of which look alike. It may require close examination, use of a hand lens and a botanical key to separate them on the basis of such botanical differences as the shape of the keel, whether twisted or straight or the number of leaflets, whether smooth or hairy. *Swainsona* grow on a variety of soils from sand plains to heavy soils; they may occur as scattered plants or in large numbers, extending over a wide area under favourable conditions. The leaves are of the feather type, with from three to numerous leaflets which are commonly greyish green and smooth to hairy; one species in the area, *S. unifoliata*, commonly has a single leaf. The typical pea

flowers may be very small to almost 1 cm and grow in sprays of different lengths. The flowers are blue to purple, or crimson with intermediate colours, and sometimes white. The seed pod is of variable size and inflated. A few examples of *Swainsona* are discussed.

S. phacoides Dwarf Swainsona. This small species with spreading to erect stems, has greyish leaves with usually 9 narrow leaflets and 6 purple, sometimes yellow or white, flowers in short spikes. This species is widely distributed and grows chiefly on sandy type soils.

S. microphylla Small Leaf Swainsona. This spreading to erect plant has variable greyish green leaves, from smooth to hairy, with up to 21 small leaflets; there are a number of small flowers in a slender spike in colours from blue to purple and yellow to white. This widespread species grows on a variety of soils from sand plains to dunes and heavy soils.

S. canescens This strong growing species grows as a large perennial, with hairy stems and long leaves, 5 to 11 cm in length; there are 9 to 17 greyish, hairy to sometimes smooth, leaflets. There are about 25 flowers, which are purple or yellow when young, crowded on a long flower spike. This species grows on sand plains throughout the area. There are two varieties, one of which is particularly toxic to sheep and cattle.

a   *Psoralea cinerea*
b   Downy Swainsona *Swainsona swainsonioides*
c   Broughton Pea *Swainsona procumbens*
d   Small Leaf Swainsona *Swainsona microphylla*
e   Batswing Coral Tree *Erythrina vespertilio*

S. swainsonioides Downy Swainsona. This is one of the more showy swainsonas and is a variable plant, forming small to large clumps with long greyish green leaves of up to 21 leaflets; the bluish to purple flowers grow in a number on a long spike. This species is found on heavier clay and loamy soils and occurs towards the north-eastern part of South Australia, but does not occur in the Northern Territory; it is common in New South Wales and Queensland.

S. procumbens Broughton Pea. This variable species is a perennial with stout, erect to prostrate stems with fine white hairs. The leaves vary from 4 to 18 cm long with from 17 to 23 greyish green leaflets; the large blue or purple flowers, 1 to 2 cm or more, have the end of the keel distinctly twisted; there are from 4 to 12 flowers on a stout stalk. This species grows on clay soils and occurs in north east South Australia and Queensland.

Glycine

This group of slender twining plants has two species in the area, one of them widespread.

G. canescens This slender twining plant has the leaf divided into 3 narrow greyish green leaflets. The small blue to purplish pea flowers grow with a number on a slender stem. The flowers are followed by cylindrical seed pods. This plant is common on sandy and rocky soils, particularly along dry watercourses where it twines over adjacent plants.

Indigofera

There are a number of different kinds of *Indigofera* with both annual and perennial types. Most are small slender plants with feathery leaves, but some have single leaves. The flowers are small, red to purple in colour, with a number on a slender flower stem; flowers are followed by slender, cylindrical seed pods. One of the larger growing species is conspicuous on rocky terrain in the Macdonnell Ranges and is discussed.

I. basedowii This bushy shrub with silvery grey foliage grows to about 1 m in height. The leaves have from 7 to 21 woolly, silvery grey, closely arranged leaflets; the small, red to purple flowers grow in short dense sprays. This species occurs on the sides of gorges and rocky hillsides.

Crotalaria

This genus is widely distributed in the warmer parts of the world; there are a number of species in the area, small herbs to shrubs, with the leaves single or divided into 3 leaflets, often with both types on the one plant. Various common names are given to these plants, such as Bird Flowers, as the flowers resemble small birds, and Rattlepod, as the inflated pods

a Indigofera basedowii
b Glycine canescens
c Crotalaria eremaea
d Crotalaria novaehollandiae
e Green Bird Flower *Crotalaria cunninghamii*
f Wallflower Poison Pea *Gastrolobium grandiflorum*

contain a number of seeds when dry and rattle when shaken. *Crotalaria* is common on sandy soils, particularly sand dunes. A few of the more widespread species are discussed.

C. novaehollandiae This species has two varieties and is usually an erect growing plant to 1 m high, with a greyish green, usually single, somewhat oblong to egg-shaped leaf; sometimes there are three leaflets; the small yellow pea flowers grow on sprays. This species is common on sand dunes.

C. eremaea An erect growing species with two varieties. The silvery grey woolly leaves have 1 to 3 leaflets; the small yellow flowers grow on long slender sprays. This species usually grows on sandy soils, particularly on dunes, although sometimes occurring on heavier red sandy loams.

C. cunninghamii Green Bird Flower. This erect woolly shrub grows to 1 m or more in height and has thick, broad, elliptical to egg-shaped, woolly, greyish leaves with one or sometimes three leaflets; the large yellowish green flowers are distinctly striped. This species is common on red sand dunes.

Gastrolobium

The common name of Poison Pea is given to this group of plants which is chiefly confined to Western Australia, with only one species in the area.

G. grandiflorum Wallflower Poison Pea. This erect shrub with oval grey-green leaves has attractive orange, red and brown flowers, with a few on a short spike; these are followed by small eliptical-shaped seed pods. This species grows in protected gorges on rocky soils along watercourses, particularly in the Macdonnell Ranges.

Acacia Family (Wattles) Mimosaceae

There are many different kinds of acacia or wattle, with numerous common names, and these form the major groups of shrubs and trees to be found in Central Australia. In view of the large number of different species, this discussion is confined to those groups which commonly occur in substantial numbers over a wide area.

Mulgas

There are a number of different mulgas, but the most widespread and abundant, especially on the red sandy loams of northern South Australia, is *Acacia aneura,* a bushy shrub to small tree with long narrow greyish leaves and yellow rodshaped flowers. This species also extends to the Northern Territory, becoming less common in northern areas. The Red Mulga or Minni Ritchi, *A. cyperophylla,* is an interesting mulga, with the trunk covered with red curly bark; this large spreading shrub to small tree has long narrow leaves; flowers are yellow in cylindrical spikes. It inhabits rocky soils, particularly along the banks of small rocky watercourses.

Western Myall This acacia,*A. papyrocarpa,* is a very attractive shrub or tree with a broad dense spreading rounded crown. It is a common wattle in the southern part of the area, often being associated with mulga and saltbush. The yellow flowerheads are globular.

Gidgees

These are sometimes called stinking wattles, as they emit an unpleasant smell during wet weather and moist evenings. There are several different gidgees all tending to larger growth and usually with a straggly appearance. Two of these are *A. cambagei* and *A. georginae* which occur chiefly on heavy clay and calcareous soils, particularly on the flood plains of the larger river systems and also along the banks of water channels. They may be widespread in suitable areas, but sometimes grow in other types of heavier soils. The Black Gidgee, *A. pruinocarpa,* prefers a different soil type to the other two species, occurring in red sands and gravels. Yellow flowerheads are globular.

A. salicina Native Willow or Cooba. Attractive pendulous willow-like wattle which occurs on various soils but prefers watercourses; pale yellow flowerheads are globular.

A. estrophiolata Ironwood. A large growing pendulous wattle which prefers sandy soils in flat areas; the pale yellow flowerheads are globular.

a Mulga *Acacia aneura*
b Gidgee *Acacia cambagei*
c Western Myall *Acacia papyrocarpa*
d Minni Ritchi *Acacia cyperophylla*
e Ironwood *Acacia estrophiolata*

a   Waddy Wood *Acacia peuce*
b   Dead Finish *Acacia tetragonaphylla*
c   Witchetty Bush *Acacia kempeana*
d   Round-leaf Wattle *Acacia strongylophylla*
e   Dune Wattle *Acacia ligulata*
f   Maitlands Wattle *Acacia maitlandii*

A. ligulata Umbrella or Dune Wattle. This acacia is a variable spreading shrub to small tree, prefering sandy soils and extending over a wide area and well into the Simpson Desert. Golden flowerheads are globular.

A. tetragonaphylla Dead Finish. A bushy shrub to small tree with pointed spiny leaves; commonly found on sandy type soils. Bright yellow flowerheads are globular.

A. kempeana Witchetty Bush. A common wattle in drier areas on sandy and rocky soils; a spreading shrub to small tree with grey oblong leaves. The aborigines obtain witchetty grubs from among the roots. Flowerheads are yellow in cylindrical spikes.

A. victoriae Elegant Wattle. This bushy wattle with spines on the stems, is a widespread species, often forming thickets, particularly near water. Pale yellow flowerheads are globular.

A. strongylophylla Round-leaf Wattle. This wattle with sharp spines on the stem has round-rhomboidal leaves with sharply pointed ends. The flowerheads are globular and bright yellow. Occurs on rocky areas and along watercourses, e.g. Standley Chasm.

A. maitlandii Maitlands Wattle. A spreading shrub to about 3 m high with small oblong, elliptical, sharply pointed leaves; the flowerheads are globular and golden. Occurs on sand and sandy loams.

A. peuce Waddy Wood. This unusual wattle with very hard wood grows to 15 m and resembles a pencil pine; the leaves are long and narrow; flower heads yellow, globular. This species is limited to a few areas in the Northern Territory and western Queensland, on sandy type soils.

Eucalyptus Family　Myrtaceae

The family Myrtaceae is represented by the various types of *Eucalyptus* species in the area, and by other genera such as the melaleucas or paperbarks which occur on water-courses and other moist areas, and smaller shrubby types of plants, such as *Micromyrtus, Thryptomene* and *Calytrix,* which occur on sandy soils and dunes or in protected rocky areas.

The Eucalypts

There are a number of different types of eucalypt in the area but they are not as widespread as the acacias, requiring a higher rainfall and soil moisture. In the southern drier parts of the area there are extensive areas of mulga (*Acacia* species), but eucalypts are confined to the beds and banks of seasonal watercourses and floodplains, where subsoil groundwater is available. As the rainfall increases, species of *Eucalyptus* occur on deeper soils with available subsoil moisture. Various common names are in use with the name gum tree being reserved for trees with a smooth single trunk, such as the River Gum. Most of the *Eucalyptus* species in the area have several slender stems or trunks arising from a woody base at ground level and are commonly known as mallees. There are a number of different kinds of mallee which vary considerably in size according to the ground moisture available. They may be shrub-like and no more than a metre in height, or may reach heights of 6 m under favourable conditions. Some of the more common species of *Eucalyptus* are discussed below.

River Red Gum

The River Red Gum, *Eucalyptus camaldulensis,* is as the common name suggests, a lover of watercourses. It is a feature of the larger seasonal watercourses, such as the Todd and Finke Rivers and Coopers Creek, where it grows in the river bed or bank, its size varying according to conditions available for growth. Although usually confined to the watercourses in favourable areas, it may extend to adjoining hills.

The River Red Gum may vary from a small slender straight to twisted tree along smaller watercourses to a very large tree with a trunk a metre or more in diameter on large watercourses, for example on the Finke River and its tributaries, the Todd River and Coopers Creek. It is an attractive tree with a smooth white to grey trunk, commonly with greyish and reddish patches, and sometimes with a layer of a white powdery bloom which may also extend to the branches. In larger trees the trunk is often rough at the base but may also be white and smooth and resemble the Ghost Gum. The narrow, greyish green, lance-shaped leaves are carried on pendulous branchlets, as are also the clusters of small white flowers.

a

b

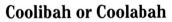

c

Coolibah or Coolabah

The Coolibah, of 'Waltzing Matilda' fame, exists as several species, of which *Eucalyptus microtheca* is the most widely distributed. It is more gregarious than the River Red Gum and is able to exist with lesser amounts of soil moisture. It occurs along shallow and larger seasonal watercourses, sometimes in association with the River Red Gum, the latter tree growing in the river beds and on the banks nearer to the source of moisture, with the coolibah higher up on the banks. The coolibah is common on the heavier soil of the floodplains of rivers such as the Diamantina and Finke. It is a small to large spreading tree with a rough, dark grey, gnarled trunk in older trees. Whilst the bark on the trunk and larger limbs is rough and dark, that on the upper branches is smooth and white to greyish. Sometimes the trunk may be smooth also, with only a rough section at the base. The leaves are greyish green and lance-shaped, and the small clusters of flowers are white.

a　Coolibah *Eucalyptus microtheca*
b　River Gum *Eucalyptus camaldulensis*
c　Ghost Gum *Eucalyptus papuana*

Ghost Gum

The Ghost Gum, *Eucalyptus papuana,* is almost synonymous with Central Australia and has been photographed more than any other type of *Eucalyptus* in the area. Albert Namatjira used the Ghost Gum as a subject in a number of his paintings. Favouring alluvial and deep sandy soils, the Ghost Gum may also grow on the side of rocky gorges, e.g. in the Macdonnell Ranges it occurs in crevices where there is a source of moisture. This graceful tree, with a slender to robust trunk, has smooth, white bark which is covered with a white powdery bloom. The bright green, lance-shaped leaves hang in a pendulous manner and contrast attractively with the white trunk and branches. The Ghost Gum extends to Western Queensland, to the north of the Northern Territory, the Kimberleys in Western Australia and to Papua in New Guinea.

Bloodwood

The Bloodwood, *Eucalyptus terminalis*, takes its common name from the red colour of the sap exudations. It is a tree which favours deeper soils where there is a readily available source of subsoil groundwater, and occurs on river flats and sandplains and similar suitable locations. It is common around Ayers Rock, where the additional water which runs off this large impervious eminence during rain provides the additional source of moisture necessary for its growth. The Bloodwood is a tall, erect to crooked, spreading tree with rough, brown, scaly bark; the leaves are thick, greyish green and lance-shaped. When in flower, usually from May to July, it produces masses of white flowers which are followed by urn-shaped seed cases.

Mallees

There are a number of different species of mallee in Central Australia. Some of these are small shrub-like plants, varying in height from less than a metre to more than 6 m, while others are trees with single trunks to 9 m. Several of the more common mallees are listed below.

Blue Mallee The Blue Mallee, *Eucalyptus gamophylla*, occurs in deep red sandy soils and on sand dunes. This mallee has a number of slender stems with rough flaky bark at the base and smooth greyish pink upper trunk and branches. The powdery, greyish green, egg- or lance-shaped leaves are usually opposite and joined at the base, the small flowers are white.

Red Mallee The Red Mallee, *Eucalyptus socialis*, grows on sandy or calcareous soils, usually on plains, but may extend to sand dunes. it may be from 2 to 9 m in height with a number of stems, or it may sometimes occur as a tree with a single trunk to 12 m. The stems or trunk are smooth and light grey, usually with the shedding strips of the old bark attached and with a rough scaly base; the leaves are narrow, lance-shaped and dull to greyish green. Other characteristics of the Red Mallee are the red colour of the branchlets and the long cap on the flower buds.

Red Bud Mallee The Red Bud Mallee, *Eucalyptus pachyphylla*, occurs on red sandy soils and sometimes dunes and is common in the Tanami Desert. It occurs both as a small shrub 1 m high, and as a mallee up to 4 m in height. The slender stems are pinkish grey, with strips of bark on the lower part of the stem; the oval-shaped leaves are greyish green and thick. An interesting feature of this mallee is the attractive red caps on the flower buds, which fall off, exposing the yellow stamens of the flowers.

a   Bloodwood *Eucalyptus terminalis*
b   *Eucalyptus gamophylla*
c   Red Mallee *Eucalyptus socialis*
d   Red Bud Mallee *Eucalyptus pachyphylla*
e   *Melaleuca viridiflora*
f   *Calytrix longiflora*
g   *Thryptomene maisonneuvei*
h   *Micromyrtus flaviflora*

Melaleucas
(Paperbarks, Tea Trees)

There are some twelve different *Melaleuca* species (commonly called paperbarks or tea trees) in the area, most of which occur in moist areas along watercourses, with some species extending to rocky hillsides. The paperbarks consist of bushy shrubs to trees, usually with papery bark, stiff leathery and mostly narrow leaves. The groups of fluffy cream to greenish flowers, with conspicuous stamens, are arranged into cylindrical or globular heads, presenting a bottle bush appearance. Many of the species are similar, and those discussed are representative of the types.

M. glomerata Inland Tea Tree. A bushy shrub, 1 to 3 m in height, with stiff dark green narrow pointed leaves; flowerheads are small, globular and pale yellow. This paperbark occurs in sandy soils in low lying areas subject to flooding.

M. dissitiflora Creek Tea Tree. A bushy shrub to 5 m in height, with dark green narrow lance-shaped leaves; flower heads are cream in loose cylindrical spikes. This paperbark occurs mostly along sandy creek beds.

M. linariifolia Tea Tree. A bushy shrub up to 5 m in height with narrow pointed dark green leaves; the creamish flowers grow in loose cylindrical spikes. This species commonly grows along the banks of watercourses.

M. viridiflora A bushy shrub to small tree, 3 to 10 m in height, with papery bark and broad greyish green elliptical leaves; the greenish flowers grow in cylindrical spikes. This species occurs in the northern part of the area along creek banks and swampy areas.

Thryptomene

There are three different thryptomenes in the area, only one of which is common. This group of twiggy shrubs have very small opposite crowded leaves. The small, white to pink flowers have 5 small spreading rounded petals and 5 calyx lobes with 5 small stamens between the petals and opposite the calyx lobes.

T. maisonneuvei A much branched shrub, 1 to 1.5 m in height, with tiny overlapping round leaves; the small white to pink flowers grow in clusters at the end of stems. This species occurs on sand dunes and is common around Ayers Rock.

Micromyrtus

There is one *Micromyrtus* in the area. It is allied to *Thryptomene,* from which it differs simply in having the 5 stamens opposite the petals.

M. flaviflora An open straggling shrub to about 1.5 m high, with tiny narrow crowded leaves. The small pink to yellowish flowers grow in clusters at the end of stems. This species occurs on gravelly and sandy soils and also in rocky gullies.

e

Calytrix

The one species of *Calytrix* in the area, *C. longiflora,* is a spreading shrub, 1 to 1.5 m in height, with small oblong crowded leaves; the pink flowers grow in clusters at the end of stems and have 5 pointed petals and 5 calyx lobes with the ends extended into awns; the calyx remains for some time after the petals have fallen. This species occurs on rocky hills and sand and gravelly plains areas.

f

h

g

Grevillea Family   Proteaceae

This family, to which the New South Wales floral emblem, the waratah, *Telopea speciosissima,* and the South African *Protea* belong, has 45 genera in Australia, only three of which occur in the area and one of which, *Persoonia,* has only one species, a shrub with small yellow tubular flowers. The other two genera, *Grevillea* and *Hakea,* are represented by a number of interesting and attractive shrubs to small trees. The flowers in the family are unusual and do not have separate petals and calyx as in most flowers. In bud the flower is tubular and splits into 4 segments which roll back, leaving an extended style which is sometimes hooked. A number of these flowers are grouped together into clusters or dense sprays. Although the flowers are similar in both *Grevillea* and *Hakea,* in the latter the seed case is hard and woody.

a *Grevillea juncifolia*
b *Grevillea wickhamii*
c *Grevillea stenobotrya*
d Beefwood *Grevillea striata*

Grevillea

There are over 250 different grevilleas, most of which are Australian and ten of these occur in the area. These species are large shrubs to small trees with flowers of cream, orange or red. Seed cases with 2 seeds commonly have the old style attached. The more common species are discussed.

G. eriostachya A bushy shrub to 3 m with branchlets and leaves finely woolly; the leaves are long and narrow, sometimes single or with up to 7 long segments; flowers are golden yellow and grow in dense, one-sided sprays, on long spreading branches; the seed case is elliptical. Occurs on dunes and sandplains. This species closely resembles *G. juncifolia,* but flowers are arranged in a more one-sided manner and style is shorter.

G. juncifolia A bushy shrub to 6 m with rough greyish bark; the long narrow leaves are single or with up to 5 long segments; new growth finely woolly and becoming smooth; flower orange in somewhat loose sprays at leaf junction or ends of branches; the seed case is egg-shaped to elliptical with the old style attached. Occurs on dunes and sandplains. This species closely resembles *G. eriostachya.*

G. stenobotrya An erect shrub to 2 m or more; leaves long and narrow; flowers white to cream in dense erect sprays. Occurs on dunes and swales between dunes.

G. striata Beefwood. A small tree to 9 m with dark grey furrowed bark; leaves narrow, up to 30 cm long; flowers cream in dense sprays. Occurs on sand plains, loam and gravel.

G. wickhamii A bushy shrub 2 to 3 m high; leaves grey, holly-like; flowers bright red in pendulous to erect sprays. Occurs on gravelly soils, rocky hills and dunes.

a

b

c

c

Hakea

There are about 150 different hakeas, all of which are Australian and of these, ten species occur in the area. These shrubs to small trees are often given common names such as Corkwood or Needlebush. The flowers closely resemble those of *Grevillea* and are white, cream and pink in colour. The seed cases are hard and woody, and open to release 2 winged seeds. The more common species are discussed.

H. chordophylla Corkwood. A small tree 3 to 7 m high with greyish, deeply furrowed bark; branchlets and leaves without hairs; leaves greyish, needle-like, up to 40 cm long; flowers cream to yellowish, smooth, in dense sprays, 8 to 16 cm long; woody fruit, egg-shaped. Occurs on red sandplains. This species resembles *H. suberea,* but foliage and flowers are without hairs.

H. eyreana A bushy shrub to small tree to 7 m with greyish, deeply furrowed bark; leaves greyish green, forked into lobes; flowers creamish yellow in dense sprays up to 10 cm long; woody fruit tapered to the apex. Occurs on red sandy loam on low lying flats and creek beds.

H. leucoptera Needlewood. A bushy shrub to small tree 7 m high with smooth grey bark; leaves needle-like, up to 9 cm long; flowers white to cream in dense sprays; woody fruit, egg-shaped, with a pointed apex. Occurs on sandy loam in low lying areas and along creeks.

H. suberea Corkwood. A small tree, 3 to 6 m high, with greyish, deeply furrowed bark; branchlets and new leaves woolly; leaves greyish green, up to 30 cm long; flowers cream,

finely woolly, in dense sprays, up to 12 cm long; woody fruit, egg- to lance-shaped, slightly curved. Occurs in red sandy soil, loams and gravels.

a Corkbark Tree *Hakea chordophylla*
b *Hakea eyreana*
c Needlewood *Hakea leucoptera*
d Corkbark Tree *Hakea suberea*

Trees

(See also Acacia, Eucalyptus, Melaleuca)

Atalaya Sapindaceae

(*See* Hopbush Family)

There are several species of *Atalaya* in Australia with one species occurring in the area. They consist of shrubs to small trees with small 5-petalled flowers and coarse, feather-shaped leaves; the fruit is winged.

A. hemiglauca Whitewood. A bushy shrub to a tree, 5 m high; the greyish green leaves have 2 to 6 pairs of smooth leaflets; flowers white in slender sprays; fruit winged. Occurs chiefly on sandy soils and in woodlands.

Whitewood *Atalaya hemiglauca*

Heterodendrum

There are four or five species in this genus in Australia with one species in the area; these shrubs with simple leaves have small flowers with 5 calyx lobes and no petals; the fruit has 2 to 4 hard globular lobes.

H. oleaefolium Rosewood, Bullocky Bush, Boonaree. A large bushy shrub to small tree to 5 m with greyish green silky, hairy, linear to narrow lance-shaped leaves, thickened at the edges; flowers small in sprays; fruit globular, with 2 to 4 lobes. Occurs on sandy soil in open woodland.

Pine and Pine-like Plants

There is one true pine or conifer in the area, White Cypress Pine (*Callitris*), and three casuarinas (now called *Allocasuarina*) which are flowering plants somewhat resembling a pine tree.

Callitris
Cupressaceae

Non-flowering small tree with small scale-like leaves, crowded on the branchlets. There are male and female cones. The female cones, which bear the seeds, become woody as they mature. There are a number of different species of *Callitris* in Australia, some of which provide the timber cypress pine.

C. columellaris (formerly known as *C. glauca*). White Cypress Pine. A small symmetrical tree about 4 m or more high; foliage dark green to greyish green; fruit cones globular, about 2 cm diameter. Occurs on rocky hillsides.

Allocasuarina
(formerly *Casuarina*)
Casuarinaceae

This family has been divided into several genera. Most of the Australian species are now known as *Allocasuarina,* with a few still known as *Casuarina.* They vary from shrubs to large trees, with tiny, close-fitting leaves around the joints of the slender branchlets. The tiny male flowers are massed at the ends of the branchlets; female flowers are in small cones which become woody and cylindrical with numerous winged seed. There are three species in the area.

A. decaisneana Desert Oak. A large attractive tree to about 15 m with rough furrowed grey bark; branches pendulous with numerous long branchlets, at the ends of which the tiny brown flowers appear; fruit large, rough, cylindrical, 2 to 6 cm or more long, 3 cm or more in diameter. Occurs on red sandy loams, sand plains and dunes. Young plants are slender and erect, appearing to be a different species from mature specimens.

Capparis Family
Capparaceae

This group of shrubs and small trees is distributed throughout the warmer parts of the world with twenty species in Australia, five

occurring in the area. These plants, which grow slowly for some time, are sprawling, tangled, spiny shrubs. As they become older they develop one or more main stems, forming a bushy shrub to small tree. The leaves are thick and tough; flowers are large with 4 to 5 soft petals and a number of stamens with stiff calyx lobes at the base; the fruit is a large globular berry at the end of a long stalk and contains a number of seeds embedded in pulp. One of the more widespread species is described.

a White Cypress Pine *Callitris columellaris*
b Wild Orange *Capparis mitchellii.*
c Desert Oak *Alocasuarina decaisneana*
d *Capparis* species

C. mitchellii Wild Orange. A bushy shrub to small dense tree with numerous branches; leaves thick, elliptical; flowers white to yellow; fruit large, 5 to 7 cm diameter, black when ripe. Widespread on heavier sandy loam and clayey loam.

50

a Desert Poplar *Codonocarpus cotinifolius*
b *Ficus platypoda*
c Berrigan *Pittosporum phylliraeoides*
d Gruie, Sour Apple *Owenia acidula*

Codonocarpus Gyrostemonaceae

This genus is one of three closely allied genera, *Didymotheca,* *Gyrostemon* and *Codonocarpus,* each with one species in the area; the first two genera are shrubs and the latter genus, *Codonocarpus,* is a widely distributed, rapid growing, short lived, slender tree, resembling a poplar. The flowers are unisexual, tiny, and without petals, having the stamens arranged in a ring; the fruit is bell-shaped.

C. cotinifolius Desert Poplar, Native Poplar, Western Bell Fruit. An erect shrub to tree, 10 m high, with growth resembling the Lombard Poplar; leaves egg-shaped to broad lance-shaped; male flowers circular in lobes; fruit bell-shaped. Occurs on red sand, sandy loam, sand plains, dunes.

Fig Family Moraceae

The Australian figs are mostly inhabitants of the east coast rainforests, where they commonly encircle other trees which they ultimately kill. The edible cultivated fig, *Ficus carica,* is commonly grown in gardens. The one species in the area is widespread and may grow as a small tree or shrub, sometimes over the surface of a rock to which it will become attached by aerial roots. The flowers are tiny with 3 to 6 minute petals; the fruit is small and fleshy.

F. platypoda A tree or shrub often with several smooth grey stems; growth may be erect, sprawling or on the surface of rock faces; leaves lance-shaped, dark green above, grey beneath; fruit round, orange to red, about 1 cm diameter. Occurs in gullies on large rocks, e.g. Ayers Rock and rock outcrops.

Cedar Family Meliaceae

A family of about 40 different genera which include many timber trees, occurs in warmer parts of the world.

Owenia

This genus with six Australian species consists of small bushy trees with milky sap, pendulous, feather-shaped leaves and small 5-petalled tubular flowers; the fruit has a fleshy outer layer. There are two species in the area.

O. acidula Gruie, Colane, Sour Apple. A small bushy spreading tree; leaves pendulous, feather-shaped, sticky with 10 to 25 lance-shaped leaflets; flowers small, brownish white in sprays; fruit globular up to 2 cm diameter, reddish; fleshy outer layer acidy and edible when ripe. Occurs on red sandy soil and dunes.

O. reticulata Desert Walnut. A small tree similar to *O. acidula,* but with leaves covered with a yellowish sticky varnish; leaflets narrower and from 4 to 12; fruit pear-shaped, red to purplish. Occurs on sandplains amongst spinifex.

Pittosporum Family Pittosporaceae

This family with nine genera extends to tropical Africa and the Pacific and is represented by eight genera in Australia, one occurring in the area. These plants, with hard fleshy leaves, have small bell-shaped flowers, followed by globular to ovoid, yellow to orange, fruit, containing sticky seeds.

P. phylliraeoides Weeping Pittosporum, Berrigan. A pendulous shrub to tree, 10 m high, with rough grey bark and long narrow leaves on pendulous branchlets; flowers small, yellowish, bell-shaped, arranged along branchlets; fruit orange, 1 to 2 cm long. Occurs on low lying areas in loamy soils and along creek beds.

Buckthorn Family Rhamnaceae

This widespread family with about 58 genera of shrubs and trees is represented in the area by three genera, each with one species.

Ventilago

This genus occurs in the warmer parts of the world and consists of trees, with one species occurring in Australia and in the area. The flowers are small without petals but with 5 calyx lobes, growing in slender sprays from the leaf junctions; the fruit is a small nut, with a long, thin wing.

V. viminalis Supple Jack. A small to medium tree, 3 to 10 m high with flexible branches, pendulous, often intertwined; the greyish green leaves are narrow to lance-shaped; flowers green to creamish yellow in slender sprays. Occurs on banks of watercourses and flood areas or in depressions.

Palms and Palm-like Plants

The one native palm in the area, *Livistona mariae,* is restricted to the deeper valleys of the Finke River and its tributaries, where there is a constant source of moisture. In addition to the native palm, the Date Palm, *Phoenix dactylifera,* has been widely planted in early settlements where there is adequate moisture. The leaves of this palm are pinnate or feather-shaped in which they differ from the palm shape of the native species.

The cycad, *Macrozamia macdonnellii,* which has a palm-like appearance, occurs in protected valleys of the Macdonnell Ranges.

The two species *Livistona mariae* and *Macrozamia macdonnellii* are relict plants, remnants of much earlier periods in the geological time scale when the climate was more equable with a high rainfall.

Livistona
Arecaceae

There are twelve different named *Livistona* in Australia with a number yet to be described.

L. mariae Cabbage Palm. A large palm with a rough ringed trunk to 20 m high; the leaves are large with a spiny leaf stalk and a broad palm-shaped blade; small, greenish-yellow flowers are produced in large numbers on large, much-branched sprays amongst the leaves; seeds round, black. Occurs only on the Finke and its tributaries in the Macdonnell Ranges. The seedling leaves of this palm are purplish red.

Top: Cycad *Macrozamia macdonnellii*
Bottom: Cabbage Palm *Livistona mariae*

Macrozamia
Zamiaceae

This genus of plants is confined to Australia with fourteen species, all of which occur on the east coast, except for one in Central Australia and the other in Western Australia. These non-flowering, male or female plants, commonly known as cycads, produce large

male or female cones; the leaves are pinnate or feather-shaped.

M. macdonnellii Cycad. A large, slow growing plant with a thick, usually underground trunk; leaves large, greyish-green, crowded at top of stem; leaflets sharply pointed; flowers absent; large male or female cones at top of plant; seeds large and nut-like in a very large cone. Occurs only in protected gullies of the Macdonnell Ranges where adequate moisture and shade is provided for part of the day.

Mistletoes, Quandongs and Others

Throughout the area there are a number of plants which attach themselves to other plants, using their host to obtain nutrients. One group, the mistletoes, have sticky seeds which are carried by mistletoe birds to the branches of other plants. Under favourable conditions, the seeds germinate and specialised roots grow into the tissues of the host plant; the mistletoe plant develops and lives as a parasite.

A further group, the quandongs, consists of large shrubs to small trees. These plants attach a number of their roots to those of other plants from which they obtain nutrients, and live a partially parasitic existence.

Another unusual parasitic plant is the Broom Rape, which has no green leaves and is parasitic on the roots of certain plants.

Mistletoe
Loranthaceae
Lysiana

There are five different *Lysianas* in the area, all growing on particular types of plants. These mistletoes have leaves, often resembling those of the host plant. The flowers are tubular, slightly swollen in the middle, usually red and green in colour, with the ends split into 6 slightly one-sided lobes. The flowers usually occur in pairs, but may be single. The fleshy fruit is globular to ellipsoid in shape.

L. subfalcata Mistletoe. A parasitic plant, with lance-shaped leaves, broadest towards the rounded or tapered apex; flowers red with green to yellow apex; fruit ellipsoid. Occurs on hosts such as *Acacia, Atalaya, Santalum, Allocasuarina.*

L. spathulata Mistletoe. A parasitic plant with flat, fleshy, spoon-shaped leaves, rounded at the top; flowers red with yellow; fruit ellipsoid, with a small nipple at the apex. Occurs on species of *Acacia, Ficus, Melaleuca* and *Eucalyptus.*

L. casuarinae Mistletoe. A parasitic plant with narrow cylindrical leaves; flowers red with green lobes; fruit ovoid. Occurs chiefly on *Casuarina* and *Acacia* species.

Amyema

These mistletoes are similar to *Lysiana,* but flowers are in groups of 3, or sometimes 2, and there are 4 to 6 lobes which commonly split to the base of the floral tube. There are nine different species in the area.

A. gibberulum Mistletoe. A parasitic plant with narrow, cylindrical, woolly, greyish leaves; flowers reddish with 4 lobes; fruit globular. Occurs only on *Hakea* and *Grevillea* species.

Quandong
Santalaceae

Santalum

These semi-parasitic shrubs to small trees, have leaves opposite or in groups; the tiny bell-shaped flowers, with 4 lobes, are followed by woody fruit with a fleshy outer covering, which is sometimes made into jam. The woody wrinkled seed case has commonly been used as marbles in the game of Chinese Checkers. The wood of some species was formerly exported to eastern countries as sandalwood, for burning as incense. There are three species in the area.

S. acuminatum Quandong. A bushy shrub to small tree with rough bark, about 6 m high; leaves lance-shaped on pendulous branches; flowers greenish yellow; fruit shiny, bright red when ripe, 2 to 5 cm diameter; flesh of fruit is edible. Occurs on sandy and loamy soils, amongst shrubs and near creeks.

S. lanceolatum Plum Bush. A bushy shrub to small tree to about 7 m; leaves lance-shaped on pendulous branches; flowers cream to pale green; fruit brownish to purplish, smooth with a round scar at the apex. Occurs on sandplains, banks of creeks and in gullies.

a   Mistletoe *Lysiana casuarinae*
b   Mistletoe *Lysiana subfalcata*
c   Mistletoe *Amyema gibberulum*
d   Quandong *Santalum acuminatum*
e   Plum Bush *Santalum lanceolatum*
f   Australian Broom Rape *Orobanche cernua* var. *australiana*

Broom Rape
Orobanchaceae
Orobanche

There is one species of this unusual parasitic plant in Australia, and it occurs in the South Australian part of the area.

O. cernua var. australiana Australian Broom Rape. A parasitic fleshy herb, without green leaves, to about 15 cm; it has a stout fleshy stem with numerous small triangular bracts from which small tubular, lobed, pinkish-purple flowers arise. Occurs in dry creek beds in South Australia.

Myoporum Family   Myoporaceae

This family of perennial plants only, with two groups *Myoporum* and *Eremophila,* is widely distributed in Central Australia

Myoporum

There are several different species of *Myoporum,* with one occurring in the Northern Territory. They consist of shrubs to small trees with fleshy, light green leaves, small, white, tubular flowers and rounded to flattened fruits, often coloured.

M. platycarpum *Sugar Wood, Sugar Tree.* A shrub to small tree to 10 m, with smooth, light green, lance-shaped leaves; the small white tubular flowers are followed by flattened seed cases. This plant exudes a resin from the branches which is sweet and sugary; hence the common name of Sugar Wood. It occurs extensively in the South Australian part of the area on sandy and stony soils.

M. acuminatum (formerly *M. montanum*) The Native Myrtle. This species is a bushy shrub, 1 to 2 m high, with fleshy light green, lance-shaped leaves; the small white, bell-shaped flowers are followed by fleshy white to purplish fruit. It occurs on sandy and stony soils in various parts of the area.

Eremophila

This group of shrubs to small trees are commonly known as Emu Bush or Poverty Bush, the former name from the habit of emus of eating the fruit, and the latter name from the fact that these plants survive in drought periods when other plants may die. There are many different kinds of *Eremophila* widely distributed throughout the drier parts of Australia. The leaves are small, long, narrow or broad, with a smooth, sticky, varnished appearance or have a covering of fine hairs. The flowers, in a wide range of colours, are bell-shaped with 4 to 5 lobes at the apex and stamens frequently projecting from the floral tube. The inner part of the flower is often spotted or hairy; frequently the calyx at the base of the flower enlarges after the floral tube falls and becomes colourful; it remains for some time becoming an attachment to the seed.

There are many different species of *Eremophila* and some of the more common, widely distributed ones are discussed.

E. duttonii A bushy shrub 1 to 3 m high, with lance-shaped, somewhat sticky leaves. The flowers are red, often marked with yellow; the stamens project and the calyx enlarges and becomes colourful after the corolla falls off. This species grows on a wide range of soil types.

E. latrobei This shrub with an open growth reaches 1 to 3 m in height; the leaves are narrow, thick, greyish green; flowers red to purplish pink, often with yellow inside; stamens project well beyond the flower; the calyx enlarges slightly after the corolla falls. This species occurs on various types of soils, often growing in association with mulga and gidgee and sometimes with spinifex.

E. maculata Native Fuchsia, Spotted Emu Bush. A variable shrub from spreading to erect and from 0.3 to 1.5 m high, with smooth to slightly hairy, narrow to broad leaves; flowers red or sometimes yellow; the inner surface of the flower is distinctly spotted and the lower lip is the longer and bent downwards; the stamens may project or be enclosed. The Native Fuchsia grows on a wide range of soils.

E. freelingii A bushy spreading shrub 1 to 2 m in height, with greyish green, soft, somewhat sticky, crowded leaves; the flowers are pale blue and the stamens do not project. This species occurs chiefly on rocky soils.

E. willsii This erect bushy shrub grows to 1 m in height; the leaves are dark green, elliptical to egg-shaped and broad or narrow; the flowers are purple, with white hairs on the upper lip. This species grows on sandy soils, often on dunes.

E. bignoniiflora This bushy shrub to small tree grows from 2 to 4 m in height, with long, narrow, drooping, greyish green leaves; the flowers are cream to yellow with brownish to purplish spotting on the lobes. This large growing Emu Bush occurs on heavy soils along rivers and creek beds.

E. christopheri An erect shrub to 2 m; leaves elliptical with pointed apex, crowded and erect; flowers blue. Occurs chiefly on rocky soils.

a Native Myrtle *Myoporum acuminatum*
b *Eremophila duttonii*
c *Eremophila christopheri*
d *Eremophila latrobei*
e Native Fuchsia *Eremophila maculata*
f *Eremophila freelingii*

a

b

c

d

e

Bignonia Family Bignoniaceae

This family of about 120 genera of mostly tropical and subtropical shrubs and trees is represented in the area by two genera, each with one species.

Pandorea

This group of erect to twining plants have the leaves divided into a number of leaflets; the flowers are bell-shaped with a 2-lobed upper lip and a 3-lobed lower lip; the fruit is an inflated pod. There is one species in the area.

P. doratoxylon Spearwood Bush. A shrub with long flexible stems up to 4 m long; leaves smooth with 5 to 9 leaflets; flowers cream with reddish brown markings and hairs in the throat. Occurs in protected rocky gullies.

a

Scrophularia Family Scrophulariaceae

This very large family of plants is widely distributed throughout the world. There are 30 Australian genera, as well as a number of naturalised species. The family includes many garden ornaments such as *Penstemon,* snapdragons (*Antirrhinum*), *Linaria,* foxglove (*Digitalis*), *Calceolaria* and many others. Many of the species are poisonous, whilst drugs are obtained from some species such as *Digitalis.* Members of the family consist of erect to creeping herbs with flowers commonly tubular with lobes. Of the eight genera in the area, two, *Mimulus* and *Stemodia,* are frequently seen.

Mimulus

There are three species of *Mimulus* in the area, all rather similar. They consist of soft, herbaceous, low growing to spreading plants with small fleshy leaves; the bell shaped flowers with 5 spreading lobes are in various shades of pink and blue to purple, often with yellow.

M. repens A prostrate, spreading, matforming plant with small egg-shaped leaves; the tubular, 2-lipped flowers are blue, mauve or pink, with 2 bumps on the lower lip. Occurs on areas subject to flooding, edges of swamps and along water-courses.

M. prostratus Similar to *M. repens,* but leaves joined at the base and flowers are without bumps on the lower lip. Occurs in similar locations to *M. repens.*

M. gracilis An erect to spreading plant, 4 to 30 cm high; leaves egg-shaped to linear oblong, edges entire to finely toothed, 0.5 to 3 cm long; flowers tubular, 2-lipped, upper lip curved back, blue, purple or pink with yellow in the tube. Occurs in low areas after flooding, swamps and creeks.

Stemodia Blue Rod
(usually regarded as including those plants known as *Morgonia*)

This genus occurs chiefly in the tropical parts of the Americas and Australia with twenty species in Australia and seven in the area. This group of herbaceous annual and perennial plants have aromatic foliage with leaves opposite or in groups of 3; the bell-shaped flowers are 2-lipped.

S. glabra Blue Rod. An erect plant with several erect stems to about 40 cm high; the fleshy, toothed, lance-shaped to narrow leaves are aromatic; flowers blue with 2 long white streaks on the lower lip. Occurs in claypans and depressed areas.

S. floribunda Blue Rod. This species closely resembles *S. glabra,* but does not have white streaks on the flower. Occurs in claypans and depressed areas.

S. viscosa A dense erect to spreading plant to 80 cm with sticky, egg-shaped to elliptical, toothed, strongly aromatic leaves; flowers purple. Occurs in protected areas on creeks, riverbeds and waterholes.

b

c

a   Spear Wood *Pandorea doratoxylon*
b   *Mimulus repens*
c   Blue Rod *Stemodia glabra*

Mint Bush Family   Lamiaceae

This large family is widespread, particularly in the Mediterranean area, and consists of herbs and shrubs, commonly with square stems, aromatic foliage and tubular, 2-lipped flowers. The family includes various exotic culinary herbs such as Mint, Thyme, Origanum and others, and many garden plants such as Ajuga, Lavender, Rosemary, Salvia, Purple Mint Bush and the like. There are about twenty genera represented in Australia and seven in the area, several of which have only one species.

a

Prostanthera

This group of shrubs has about 85 species in Australia and several in the area. The plants have aromatic foliage, smooth, opposite leaves; bell-shaped flowers, distinctly 2-lipped, with an upper and lower lip and 2-lobed calyx; they grow in short sprays.

P. striatiflora Mint Bush. An erect bushy shrub, 1 to 2 m high; flowers white, marked with yellow spots in the throat and purple striping on the lips. Occurs mostly in protected rocky gullies.

Plectranthus

This group of plants occurs in the warmer parts of the world with some seventeen species in Australia, one of which occurs in the area. These herbaceous plants with fleshy stems and leaves have small violet to blue, two-lipped flowers growing in long slender sprays at the ends of stems.

P. intraterraneus A soft square stemmed erect aromatic plant 60 cm to 1 m high; leaves egg-shaped, fleshy, greyish green, coarsely toothed or entire; flowers violet, in slender sprays. Occurs in rocky gullies and creek beds.

Teucrium

This group of shrubs and herbs occurs in the warmer parts of the world and some are

a *Plectranthus intraterraneus*
b *Teucrium racemosum*
c Mint Bush *Prostanthera striatiflora*
d *Rostellaria pogonanthera*

cultivated as garden plants. There are nine or ten Australian species with two species in the area. The flowers, with 5 calyx lobes, have a short floral tube in the lower part and the upper section spreads out into 5 lobes, with the pistil and stamens projecting.

T. racemosum A slender, erect to spreading plant to about 50 cm high with 4-angled stems; leaves narrow, oblong to egg-shaped; flowers white in slender sprays. Occurs on heavy clay soils.

Acanthus Family   Acanthaceae

Rostellaria

This genus belongs to the large family Acanthaceae which is found chiefly in tropical parts of the world from rainforests to arid zones. It includes many commonly cultivated garden plants such as *Thunbergia* and *Beloperone*. The genus *Rostellaria* consists of herbs, with dense spikes of short bell-shaped flowers with an upper and lower lip. The one species in the area extends to other states.

R. pogonanthera A soft plant with a number of stems to about 40 cm high with soft, hairy, greyish green, elliptical leaves; flowers pink to purple in dense spikes. Occurs on red sandy soil, alluvials, clays, gibber plains and stony hills.

Verbena Family   Verbenaceae

This large family of plants is widely distributed throughout the world and includes herbs, shrubs, trees and twining plants with tubular, often 2-lipped flowers. The family includes timber trees and numerous garden plants, such as *Verbena, Clerodendrum.*

There are two genera in the area, *Clerodendrum* and *Verbena,* the three species of *Verbena* being all naturalised plants.

Clerodendrum

This group of shrubs and twining plants, which occurs in tropical and sub-tropical areas, have tubular flowers with 5 spreading lobes and projecting stamens; the calyx enlarges when the petals have fallen. The genus includes a number of attractive, exotic, cultivated garden plants such as the Blue Butterfly Shrub, *Clerodendrum ugandense.* There are two species in the area.

C. floribundum A large shrub to small tree with smooth, egg-shaped to elliptical leaves; flowers white; fruit with purplish seeds and fleshy, enlarged, reddish purple calyx lobes. Occurs on heavier type soils with ample moisture.

C. tomentosum Similar to *C. floribundum,* but the leaves and flower stalks are softly hairy.

a

Chloanthes Family   Chloanthaceae

This family is closely allied to the Verbena family, with which is was formerly included. There are four genera in the area which are small to medium sized shrubs with woolly foliage. Two of the genera are more widely distributed.

Dicrastylis

This group of softly hairy shrubs have small woolly tubular flowers with five lobes and the style deeply forked; the flowers are arranged in groups or spikelike sprays. There are a number of different species in the area with several subspecies and varieties.

D. exsuccosa An erect shrub 1 m or more high with soft hairy stems and lance-shaped leaves; flowers with yellow brown hairs on the inside and white smooth spreading lobes. Occurs in rocky gullies and sandy areas.

Newcastelia

This genus is closely allied to Dicrastylis, but differs in the style being entire or only slightly but not deeply forked; the leaves are woolly or hairy and flowers are in dense, terminal spikes, or sub-globular heads.

N. bracteosa A grey woolly plant with a number of erect stems; leaves crowded, soft grey, oblong to lance-shaped; flowers in dense greyish purple spikes. Occurs on sand and sandy loam.

a   *Clerodendrum floribundum*
b   *Newcastelia bracteosa*
c   *Dicrastylis exsuccosa*

b

c

Blue Bell Family   Campanulaceae

This family of plants occurs in the temperate and sub-tropical parts of the world and consists of herbs which have a white sap; the flowers are bell-shaped with spreading lobes, sometimes with the tube split on one side; the seed cases are urn-like with numerous small seeds. The family includes a number of cultivated garden plants such as *Campanula* and *Lobelia.*

Wahlenbergia

A group of soft annual plants with a number of different forms from very small to large flowered types, often difficult to separate from one another, with a number still unnamed. Flowers are bell-shaped with widely spreading lobes; seed capsules small, urn-shaped with numerous fine seed.

W. communis Blue Bell. A slender plant with a number of slender, erect to spreading stems; leaves slightly hairy, linear to narrow elliptical; flowers blue. Occurs chiefly on sandy loam.

a

Isotoma

A group of prostrate to erect herbs with much-branched stems and toothed or lobed leaves; the sap is white and acrid and should be handled carefully, as it causes pain if it reaches the eyes or mouth; the flowers are tubular with 5 spreading lobes and a tube notched on one side; fruit a small, urn-shaped capsule with fine seed. There are two species in the area.

I. petraea Rock Isotoma. A slender, much-branched plant with leaves coarsely toothed or lobed; flowers tubular, white to blue, with 5 spreading lobes, tubes notched on one side.

b

W. gracilis Blue Bell. A small variable species similar to *W. communis,* but generally smaller in all parts. Occurs chiefly on sandy loam.

Occurs on rocky hills and outcrops, often in crevices of rocks.

Goodenia Family   Goodeniaceae

This family extends to New Guinea and Indonesia and consists of perennial herbs or shrubs. The family includes the well known Blue Lechenaultia from Western Australia. The lower part of the flowers is tubular and split almost to the base on one side; there are 5 broad lobes spread out in hand-like manner. The column-like style has a cap or cover known as an indusium. There are five genera in the area, three of which are well represented.

Goodenia

There are about 170 different species of *Goodenia* with two extending to New Guinea and about 28 occurring in the area, many of which appear to be very similar. This group of shrubs to erect or prostrate herbs, have alternate leaves, but in the herbaceous species they are usually at the base of the plant and often on the flowering stem. The flowers are chiefly yellow, with some white and blue, shortly tubular in the lower part and split almost to the base on one side; there are 5 lobes with thin membranous edges or wings, with 3 lower lobes and usually 2 upstanding;

the style and indusium are simple or divided. Two examples of the genus are described.

G. pinnatifida A variable spreading to erect plant; coarsly-toothed to lobed leaves, oblong to broad lance-shaped in outline; flowers yellow. Occurs on sand dunes and sandy soils. This species is typical of a number in the area.

G. grandiflora An erect to spreading plant with egg-shaped to almost round, coarsely toothed, sticky leaves; flowers white to bluish, marked with distinct stripes. Occurs on protected rocky slopes.

Scaevola

This group of spreading to erect herbs or shrubs takes its name from the Roman soldier Scaevola, who, to show his disregard for pain, placed his hand into a fire and let it burn. The flowers, with a tube split on one side, have 5 lobes spread out in the manner of a hand. There are seven different species in the area.

S. depauperata A spreading shrub to about 60 cm; leaves mostly small, narrow to lance-shaped; flowers blue to cream. Occurs on sand dunes.

S. ovalifolia A spreading variable plant to about 60 m high; leaves oblong to round; flowers pale blue. Occurs on sandy and rocky soils.

Dampiera

This group of small herbs and shrubs with about 65 species is confined to Australia. The flowers, usually blue, somewhat resemble *Scaevola,* but the 3 lower lobes are winged and the 2 upper lobes have 2 small ear-like lobes which enclose the indusium; the stamens unite around the style.

D. cinerea A spreading woolly shrub to 80 cm with close greyish hairs; leaves hairy, narrow oblong to narrow elliptical; flowers purplish-blue. Occurs on sand plains and dunes.

a   Bluebell *Wahlenbergia gracilis*
b   Rock Isotoma *Isotoma petraea*
c   *Goodenia grandiflora*
d   *Goodenia* species
e   *Scaevola ovalifolia*

c

d

e

Brunonia Family   Brunoniaceae

a

There is only one species in this family, *Brunonia australis,* which is widespread throughout temperate Australia. This annual or perennial herb, with leaves at ground level, has small tubular flowers with 5 spreading lobes, with a large number grouped into a head.

B. australis Blue Pincushion. A small plant, with soft, hairy, lance-shaped leaves, grouped together at ground level; flowerheads globular, blue with yellow stamens. Occurs on various soils, but chiefly on sandy types.

Stackhousia Family Stackhousiaceae

b

This family of two genera, *Macgregoria* and *Stackhousia,* are represented in the area and are herbaceous plants with small flowers.

Macgregoria

These small annual plants with only one species are confined to the arid parts of Australia. Following heavy rains, they grow rapidly from seed, quickly becoming compact plants with masses of small white flowers in such profusion as to cover the foliage.

M. racemigera Snow Flower. A small compact plant 3 to 15 cm high; leaves linear, tiny; flowers small, white, with 5 petals in slender sprays above leaves. Ocurs on red sand, sandy loam and stony soils, often in depressions.

Kurrajong Family   Sterculiaceae

This family of trees, shrubs and perennial herbs has some 1100 different species in tropical and subtropical parts of the world and includes a number of Australian species, some of them with attractive flowers. The family is best known in Australia by the large rainforest tree, the Flame Tree *Brachychiton acerifolium* and the kurrajong *Brachychiton populneum.* There are a number of important plants in the family such as *Theobroma cocoa* from Central America which provides cocoa, and *Cola vera* and *C. acuminata* from West Africa which provide cola.

Brachychiton

There are twelve species in this genus of small to large trees which are endemic to Australia. The leaves are entire or lobed in a finger-like manner. The flowers, without petals, are male or female and have a coloured petal-like calyx in a bell shape with 5 lobes; the fruit is tough, woody and boat-shaped. One species occurs in the area.

B. gregorii Desert Kurrajong. A small compact tree with large leaves, deeply 3 to 5 lobed, which become deciduous during dry periods; flowers small, bell-shaped, pale cream with red, woolly outside, in small sprays; fruit ovoid. Occurs chiefly on sand dunes.

Keraundrenia

There are two species of this genus in the area, consisting of shrubs with hairy fleshy leaves; the flowers are without petals but the calyx is enlarged, coloured and petal-like.

K. integrifolia A bushy shrub to about 1 m with oblong leaves, greenish above and greyish beneath; flowers violet to blue with 5 petal-like calyx lobes. Occurs on red sandy soils and rocky hillsides.

a Blue Pincushion *Brunonia australis*
b Snow Flower *Macgregoria racemigera*
c *Keraudrenia integrifolia*

c

59

Rulingia

This group of prostrate to erect shrubs, with about seventeen Australian species, has three species in the area. The leaves are rough, entire or lobed; flowers have 5 petals and 5 calyx lobes similar in colour to the petals. The most attractive species in the area is *Rulingia magniflora*.

R. magniflora An erect shrub to about 2 m with velvety foliage; the leaves are oblong to lance-shaped, shallowly toothed; flowers pink with 5 spreading petals and calyx lobes, woolly outside. Occurs in protected, part-shaded, rocky gullies.

Frankenia Family   Frankeniaceae

This genus is one of four genera which form the family Frankeniaceae, found in tropical and subtropical parts of the world. This group of salt loving plants, with one genus in Australia, are herbs or small shrubs with small leaves; the flowers have 4 to 6 calyx lobes and petals and are chiefly pink in colour. There are a number of species in the area, many of which are similar in appearance.

F. cordata A small spreading to clump-forming plant with small, heart-shaped to egg-shaped leaves; flowers pink, 6-petalled. Occurs around the margins of saltpans, salt lakes and in saline soils.

Carrot Family   Apiaceae

Trachymene

This genus belongs to the same family as the vegetable carrot *Daucus,* parsnip *Pastinaca* and celery *Apium*. Many members of the family are poisonous. This group of herbs, with a thickened tap root, frequently have a strong odour; the leaves on long stalks are deeply divided; flowers are small, 5-petalled and arranged in pincushion-like heads. There are 4 species in the area, some of which are known to be toxic to stock.

T. glaucifolia Blue Parsnip, Wild Carrot. An erect annual to 60 cm or more high, with a thickened taproot; leaves divided deeply into 3 to 5 main lobes; flowers numerous, white to violet. Occurs on sandy loam, sand and gravel, often amongst spinifex and mulga.

Saltbush Family   Chenpodiaceae

The saltbush family of plants is particularly adapted to growing in dry areas in soils which are saline or alkaline, such as calcareous types of soil. The saltbushes are well represented in other parts of the world under similar conditions to those found in Central Australia. There are a number of different types of plants in the saltbush family with both annual and perennial species, all of which have the capacity to grow under conditions unfavourable to many types of plants. Although representatives are found throughout Australia, the greatest concentration occurs in the southern part of the area in the wide spread calcareous and saline soils. In such areas the saltbush group may be dominant, covering large areas and frequently occurring as an understorey beneath larger plants such as mulga (see 'Acacias'). The saltbushes are a useful fodder plant for stock. Various common names are applied to different groups of these plants; however, the common name of saltbush is frequently used broadly to cover all the groups. There are a number of different genera, but for a simple understanding, they may be placed into four main groups as follows:

1. Saltbushes Although, as mentioned previously, the common name of saltbush is applied to a number of groups, the genera *Atriplex, Chenpodium, Rhagodia* and

a

c

e

d

a   Rulingia magniflora
b   Frankenia cordata
c   Saltbush *Atriplex*
d   Saltbush *Rhagodia nutans*
e   Pop Saltbush *Atriplex holocarpa*

Enchylaena are usually regarded as the saltbushes. These plants, which may be low-growing types to large shrubs 2 m high, have mostly flat, somewhat fleshy, greyish green leaves which may glisten beneath with salt crystals. The seeds (fruit) may be spongy, hard and fleshy or berry like. Plants sometimes have a cottony appearance and may be called Cottonbush. These plants tend to favour weakly saline and alkaline and heavy clayey soils.

2. Bluebushes This group take the common name of Bluebush from the bluish grey hoary appearance they frequently present, whilst some have a cottony appearance and may be called Cottonbush. This group of plants are known as *Maireana* (formerly known as *Kochia*). The Bluebushes have thick narrow fleshy leaves with a bluish grey hoary or cottony appearance and may grow up to 1 m in height. The shiny seeds (fruit) have spreading membranous wings with colours of yellow, pink or red. These plants favour calcareous soils and are very common in the southern part of the area, particularly where the Bluebush *M. sedifolia* is widely distributed.

3. The Burrs such as Copperburr, Galvanised Burr, Goathead Burr, Bindy Eye The names mentioned are some of the many common names applied to members of this group. Many of the species which look very much alike and require close examination to separate were formerly included under a large group known as *Bassia*. Botanists have now divided this genus into several different groups with one large group *Scleroleana* and smaller groups, *Neobassia, Dissocarpus, Sclerochlamys.* This group of usually lowgrowing spreading plants have small, fleshy, hoary, greyish leaves and tiny flowers. The seeds have a woolly appearance with hairs which cover several sharp stiff spines. When ripe, the seeds fall to the ground, where they remain for an indefinite period until conditions for germination occur. The seeds present a problem, particularly for campers, and can render a site unsuitable for camping. They occur on various types of soil, particularly harder stony ones.

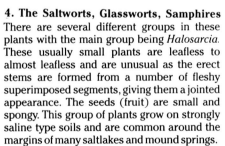

4. The Saltworts, Glassworts, Samphires There are several different groups in these plants with the main group being *Halosarcia.* These usually small plants are leafless to almost leafless and are unusual as the erect stems are formed from a number of fleshy superimposed segments, giving them a jointed appearance. The seeds (fruit) are small and spongy. This group of plants grow on strongly saline type soils and are common around the margins of many saltlakes and mound springs.

a　Ruby Saltbush *Enchylaena tomentosa*
b　Bluebush *Maireana sedifolia*
c　Cannon Ball *Dissocarpus paradoxa*
d　Copper Burr *Sclerolaena limbata*
e　Samphire *Halosarcia pruinosa*
f　Bluebush *Maireana georgei*
g　Lignum *Muehlenbeckia cunninghamii*

Polygonum Family　　Polygonaceae

This family is spread throughout the world and includes a number of weeds, such as the various dock weeds. There are four genera in the area all with small flowers, but one introduced species, *Rumex vesicarius,* has conspicious fruit.

Muehlenbeckia

A group of erect to climbing plants with numerous, often tangled stems, and small leaves which are often absent; flowers small, white to cream, in clusters. The genus extends to New Zealand and South America. There are three species in the area.

M. cunninghamii Lignum. An erect spreading shrub, 2 to 4 m high with numerous tangled, often spiny, stems, forming a dense mass; the leaves when present are small and narrow; flowers cream, inconspicuous. Occurs commonly on low lying, heavy, clayey soils subject to flooding, in claypans and swamps and along the banks of watercourses. In some flood areas this plant forms almost impenetrable masses, extending over wide areas and forming lignum swamps.

Rumex
Dock Weed

This genus is widely distributed throughout the world and is a common weed on cultivated land, particularly where badly drained. The two native species in the area have inconspicuous flowers. There is an introduced species, *Rumex vesicarius,* from Northern Africa and Western Asia, which is rapidly spreading through the area, particularly the Macdonnell Ranges. As it is of use for stock fodder and the fruits are colourful, no action is being taken to prevent its spread, unfortunately.

Rumex vesicarius Rosy Dock. An erect introduced annual plant with a number of fleshy stems and egg-shaped leaves; flowers small, reddish, in spikes, followed by inflated, bright pink, hop-like fruit. Widespread in various areas, particularly in rock crevices.

Cucumber Family   Cucurbitaceae

The cucumber family is widely distributed throughout the warmer parts of the world and is an important source of food. It includes the forms and varieties of *Cucumis melo* from which different forms of rock melons have been developed, *Cucumis sativus* the cucumber with its different forms, and *Citrullus lanatus* from which watermelons and pie melons have been developed. The list could go on and on from pumpkins to gourds and even vegetable sponges, *Luffa cylindrica.* This group of climbing plants with tendrils has five genera in Australia, some species of which are naturalised, but most, except for some *Mukia* species, extending to other parts of the world, such as Africa, Asia and the Mediterranean. A number of the species have small fruit which are not commonly observed. Three of the more common species with larger fruit are discussed.

Citrullus lanatus Wild, Bitter or Bastard Melon. A spreading plant with deeply lobed leaves; fruit almost globular, up to 15 cm diameter, green mottled with white. A widespread species along roadsides, watercourses and in moist depressions. A naturalised species from South Africa.

Cucumis melo subspecies ***agrestis*** Icardo melon. A spreading plant with lobed leaves; fruit ovoid to elliptical/oblong, smooth or hairy, greenish, up to 4 cm long. Occurs along watercourses, extends to Asia and Africa.

Cucumis myriocarpus Paddy Melon, Gooseberry Cucumber. Similar in growth to the former species, but fruit almost globular with soft bristles, darker and lighter green bands turning yellow. Occurs in depressions where moisture is available. Naturalised from South Africa.

Asclepias Family   Asclepiadaceae

Sarcostemma

This genus belongs to a large family which occurs in the warmer parts of the world. It includes a number of garden ornamentals such as *Stephanotis* and *Hoya.* The genus *Sarcostemma* occurs in Africa and New Caledonia; there are one or two species in Australia, with one in the area.

S. australe Caustic Vine, Milk Bush. An unusual scrambling, twining to pendulous plant, with fleshy, long, greyish green stems containing a milky sap, appearing to be leafless, but with minute leaves; flowers tiny,

white, with 5 lobes in clusters; fruit a cylindrical follicle containing seeds with silky hairs. Occurs on stony soils, rocky hills, amongst acacias in protected positions.

Left: Caustic Vine *Sarcostemma australe*
Above: Paddy Melon *Cucumis myriocarpus* and
Rosy Dock Rumex vesicarius

Hop Bush Family   Sapindaceae

This family of trees, shrubs and twining plants, usually with small flowers and interesting different types of fruit, occurs chiefly in the warmer parts of the world and includes a number of valuable timber trees and edible fruits such as the Chinese Leechee or Lychee, *Litchi chinensis,* as well as cultivated garden plants. There are four genera in the area, two of which are represented by only one species each, the Whitewood *Atalaya hemiglauca* and Rosewood *Heterodendrum oleaefolium,* both small trees. Another genus, *Diplopeltis,* is a small shrub with small 4-petalled flowers; the fourth genus, *Dodonaea,* has six species in the area.

Dodonaea

This group of shrubs, often with sticky foliage, have small flowers with 4 sepals but no petals; sometimes the plants are either male or

b

c

female; the fruit is a 3 to 4 winged capsule, resembling the hop used for brewing beer. Early settlers are said to have used the fruit for this purpose, hence the common name of hopbush. The genus is widely distributed in Australia with 61 different species and six in the area.

D. lanceolata Hopbush. An erect shrub, 1 to 2 m high, with elliptical leaves with thickened

edges; flowers tiny, fruit 3-winged, reddish. Occurs in open woodlands, on rocky hills and along watercourses.

D. petiolaris Hopbush. An erect shrub, 1 to 2 m high, with smooth sticky, lance-shaped to egg-shaped leaves; flowers tiny; fruit large, mottled pink, 3-winged and much inflated. Occurs in mulga, gibber plains, rocky hills and ranges.

D. viscosa* var. *spatulata Hopbush. A bushy shrub, 1 to 2 m high, with leaves shaped like a spatula with a blunt top and often with a small point; flowers tiny; fruit 3- to 4-winged but not inflated as in *D. petiolaris.* Occurs on rocky hills and ranges.

Zygophyllum Family   Zygophyllaceae

This family of plants which is found in tropical and sub-tropical parts of the world consists of herbs to shrubs, often with yellow flowers. There are four genera in the area.

T. occidentalis Bullhead. A prostrate perennial herb with greyish-green, hairy, opposite leaves; flowers yellow, to 2.5 cm diameter; fruit with short, hard spines. Occurs on sandy and stony soils and dunes.

a Hopbush *Dodonaea lanceolata*
b Hopbush *Dodonaea viscosa*
c Hopbush *Dononaea petiolaris*
d Bullhead *Tribulus occidentalis*
e Clasping Twin-leaf *Zygophyllum howittii*

Nitraria

This genus, which extends from the Sahara to Russia, consists of shrubs, often spiny, with small leaves and small, 5-petalled flowers. The flowers are followed by fleshy or hard fruits. There is one species in Australia, which extends from coastal sand dunes to Central Australia.

N. billardiera Nitre Bush. A stiff, bushy, tangled, spreading, often spiny shrub, 1 to 2 m high, with small, lance-shaped, hairy leaves; flowers white in clusters; fruit fleshy, 1 to 2 cm long, red, purple or orange when ripe, edible. Occurs in claypans and saline and calcareous soils along creeks.

Zygophyllum

This group of mainly annuals occurs in desert and arid areas of South Africa and from Central Asia to the Mediterranean. There are about twenty different species in Australia, twelve of which occur in the area. These plants have fleshy leaves which are usually 2-lobed, thence the common name of Twin-leaf. The flowers have 3 to 5 soft yellow petals, which are followed by angular, 3- to 4-winged fruit, resembling hops. A number of the species appear to be very similar. One of the common species is described.

Z. howittii Clasping Twin-leaf. A spreading to clump-forming annual with fleshy leaves, distinctly lobed at the apex; flowers small, with 3 yellow petals; fruit 3-winged, purplish. Occurs on dunes and rocky areas.

Tribulus

This group of plants with ten Australian species are annual to perennial herbs with feather-shaped leaves. The large flowers have 5 spreading, yellow petals and a number of stamens. These soft buttercup-like flowers are followed by spiny fruit and, for people camping in an area where they grow freely, their presence is unpleasant. There are six species in the area which are very similar in appearance and require ripened fruit to separate.

d

e

Ferns

In protected, shaded, moist gullies and waterholes, different fern species may occur. Some of the hardier types which are able to die down during dry periods are the Rock Ferns *Cheilanthes* and the unusual clover-like fern *Marsilea*; these two groups are discussed.

Cheilanthes Adiantaceae

A group of small ferns with somewhat coarse fronds. They commonly occur in the crevices of rocks along water-courses and gorges, but may also occur amongst mulga *(Acacia)* in moist situations. These ferns become brown and dry during dry periods, rapidly coming to life after rain. There are four species in the area.

C. tenuifolia Rock Fern. A small fern with slightly hairy fronds 10 to 20 cm, with 3 to 4 pairs of leaflets or pinnae. Occurs in rocky protected positions or moist shaded areas.

C. lasiophylla Woolly Cloak Fern. A small fern with woolly fronds to about 15 cm; fronds

a

covered in brown hairs. Occurs in the crevices of rocks such as Ayers Rock and the Olgas.

Marsilea Marsileaceae

This group of unusual ferns with the common name of nardoo have fronds with four leaflets, resembling clover. Unlike most ferns which produce spores on the back of the fronds, nardoo have their spores in small inflated spore cases at the base of the frond stalk. These ferns grow as aquatic plants or may occur in soils which become flooded during rain. There are four species in the area.

M. drummondii Common Nardoo. A much-branched species with extensive creeping

b

stems; fronds 20 to 30 cm with greyish to brownish, hairy to smooth leaflets; spore cases on a distinct stalk. A common species on heavier, moist, flat areas, subject to flooding.

M. hirsuta Short Fruit Nardoo. A species with creeping stems; leaflets widely spaced, greenish to brownish, frequently with scalloped edges. Spore cases on very short stalks. Prefers positions where water remains as pools for some time, with leaflets floating on the surface of water or projecting.

M. mutica A mainly aquatic plant with leaves commonly floating on surface of water or projecting; leaflets with two coloured greens separated by a brown band. Spore case in groups or single, on a short stalk. Occurs in areas where water remains as a pond for a period.

Grasses

There are many different kinds of grasses throughout the area with innumerable common names and of both annual and perennial types. In addition to the native species of grass there are many introduced exotic species, such as Buffel Grass, *Cenchrus ciliaris,* which has become naturalised. Grasses commonly grow in association with other plants, but they may be the dominant form of growth in an area.

During dry periods, the perennial grasses (with the exception of spinifex) may become brown and appear to be dead, but, after rain, soon produce new growth. Annual grasses grow rapidly from seed after rain, quickly reach maturity, produce seed and then die, to await the next period of rain to repeat the process. Various types of grass look very much

alike and, with so many different types, are often difficult to separate without considerable experience.

The grasses in the area have two distinct forms of growth and are commonly known as: 1. Tufted, Tussock or Bunch Grass and 2. Hummock or Mound-forming Grass.

1. Tufted, Tussock or Bunch Grass

This form of grass grows as distinct tufts or bunches with a number of stems and leaves arising from the base. Unlike the many spreading coastal grasses which may cover the area in which they are growing, plants of

Tufted or Bunch Grass may be from 30 to 90 cm apart. In favourable seasons the spaces between the tufts are covered with annual plants, such as daisies, and other soft herbaceous types. In areas of overgrazing, these may actually replace the grasses.

The seeds of many grasses have sharp bristles or awns, barbs and fine toothing on the seed husks or cases. Frequently the extended bristle on the seed is twisted and bent, characteristics which, with wind action, assist in distribution of the seed, also enabling it to twist itself into the soil. The fine barbs on the seed become attached to passing objects. Those who have walked through inland grasses will have experienced the discomfort of grass seeds becoming attached to clothing and, with movement, working their way through the material into the skin.

With so many different grasses which are difficult to separate and identify, only a few of the more widespread, more commonly named groups are discussed. For those who would like to know more, it is necessary to consult technical works on the subject.

Kangaroo Grass

There are two species of Kangaroo Grass in the area, one of which, *Themeda australis,* is

c

d

a Rock Fern *Cheilanthes tenuifolia*
b Nardoo *Marsilea hirsuta*
c Buffel Grass *Cenchrus ciliaris*
d Kangaroo Grass *Themeda australis*

distributed throughout Australia, even extending to Papua New Guinea. This leafy grass grows to about one metre or more in height and has loose seed heads, with long twisted and bent extensions on the seed. *Themeda avenacea* differs chiefly from *T. australis* in its more robust habit of growth. Kangaroo Grass favours the banks of creeks and protected areas.

Flinders Grass

There are a number of different kinds of Flinders Grass, all of which belong to the genus *Iseilema* and are chiefly annuals or short-lived perennials. Flinders Grasses are generally leafy, reddish brown to purplish in colour, loose to compact, tufted grasses with a leafy seed head.

The small Rough Stemmed Flinders Grass, *I. dolichotrichum,* grows to only 15 cm high, in contrast to Bull Flinders Grass, *I. macrantherum,* which may reach about one metre; this latter species occurs in the northern part of the area. The widely distributed Red Flinders Grass, *I. vaginiflorum,* is a leafy, annual, spreading, reddish purple grass, which grows to about 60 cm in height. Flinders Grass usually grows on cracking clay and the heavier alluvial soils, sometimes in association with Mitchell Grass.

Mitchell Grass

There are four different species of Mitchell Grass in the area, all of which belong to the genus *Astrebla.* These drought resistant perennial grasses form slender to coarse, compact, erect to spreading, leafy tufts or tussocks, usually with branched stems; seed heads are on long stems and are tightly packed. The species are: Curly Mitchell Grass, *A. lappacea;* Barley Mitchell Grass, *A. pectinata,* with seed heads resembling those of barley; Hoop, Slender or Weeping Mitchell Grass, *A. elymoides,* with long slender seed stems which bend over; Bull Mitchell Grass, *A. squarrosa,* the largest growing species, up to 1.5 m in height. Mitchell Grass is widely distributed and occurs on heavy clay soils, particularly on flood plains.

Mulga Grass

There are several different Mulga Grasses, all in the family Neurachneae, but with several different genera, e.g. Dwarf Mulga Grass *Neurachne munroi,* Window Mulga Grass *Thyridolepis mitchelliana,* and Northern Mulga Grass *Paraneurachne muelleri.* These perennial grasses form leafy tufts or tussocks 15 to 50 cm in height and have closely packed seed heads. Mulga Grass prefers red sandy type soils and is common on sandplains, often growing in association with mulga *(Acacia).*

Speargrass

There are a number of different genera of grasses to which the common name of Speargrass is applied. Two of the larger genera are *Stipa* and *Aristida* (this genus is also given other common names, see below). The seeds

of both groups have a sharp pointed base, and in the case of *Stipa* there is a long bristle extension which is spirally twisted or bent; hence the common name of Corkscrew Grass which is sometimes used. *Stipa* species grow in slender bunches, to large erect to spreading tufts, with loose seed heads. These grasses grow in a range of soils, from clays to sandy and rocky soils.

Wire Grass, Three Awn Grass, Spear Grass

The genus *Aristida* has a number of different annual or perennial species with various common names. These grasses grow as erect to spreading tufts or bunches, with loose seed heads in which the awns project from the seed cases. The seed has a sharp pointed base and the apex terminates in 3 bristly awns. The members of this large genus grow on a wide variety of soils from cracking clay soils, claypans and sandplains to dunes and steep rocky hillslopes. Two common widespread species are *A. latifolia,* Feathertop Wire Grass and *A. contorta,* with various common names such as Wind Grass, Sand Wire Grass, Spear Grass or Bunched Kerosene Grass. Both species form tufts or tussocks and have 3 long bristly awns surmounting a twisted extension. The former species grows on plains of clayey soil and the latter on sandplains and dunes.

A. **browniana** Erect Kerosene Grass. This erect tufted grass with 3 long awns on the seed similar to *A. contorta* is widespread particularly on coarse sandy soils.

Nine Awn Grass

This group of annual and perennial grasses belong to the genus *Enneapogon,* commonly known as Nine Awn, from the nine spreading awns attached to the top of the seeds. The species consist of slender, tufted, usually hairy plants, with a compact seed head, with distinct projecting awns. There are eight different species in the area, three of which are widely distributed; these are Leafy Nine Awn,

a Mitchell Grass
b Erect Kerosene Grass
c Flinders Grass
d Bristly Love Grass

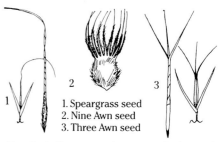

1. Speargrass seed
2. Nine Awn seed
3. Three Awn seed

E. polyphyllus, a dense, tufted, leafy, somewhat sticky plant to 45 cm high, with a short close dense seed head; Oat Nineawn or Bottle Washers, *E. avenaceus,* a small hairy plant, 15-30 cm, with tufted seed heads; Jointed Nineawn, *E. cylindricus,* a slender tufted plant to 20 cm with a slender, elongated, cylindrical, fragile seed headed.

Love Grass

This large genus *Eragrostis* takes its common name from the generic name which means Love Grass. The genus is widespread in Australia with many different species of both annual and perennial types, including naturalised exotic species. Some of the coarse growing types are known as Cane or Bamboo Grass, for example, *E. australasica,* a tall erect growing perennial grass which may reach 3 m in height and is commonly known as Swamp Cane Grass, Tall Canegrass or Bamboo Grass. It grows on claypans and areas subject to intermittent flooding, such as swamps and slightly saline areas.

Love Grass generally grows as slender tufts to large, leafy, dense tussocks and the seed heads have flattened spiklets with closely packed seed. In contrast to the large growing *E. australasica,* Neat Lovegrass *E. basedowii,* is a small annual tufted plant from 7 to 25 cm high. Love Grass grows on various types of soil from sand to heavy clay, favouring low lying areas subject to flooding.

Sand Hill Cane Grass

Common on sand dunes, particularly in the Simpson Desert, the Sand Hill Cane Grass, *Zygochloa paradoxa*, grows as a robust perennial grass with thick stems. It forms dense tangled tussocks to 1.5 m with the seed heads in clusters.

2. Hummock or Mound Forming Grasses

The common name of spinifex is given to those groups of perennial grasses which have a distinct hummock or mound form of growth, from which the seed heads develop, growing well above the hummock and presenting an attractive appearance. There are two genera which develop the hummock form of growth. *Triodia*, the larger genus, and *Plectrachne*, the latter differing from *Triodia* chiefly in the more open growth of the seed heads, the longer extension of the seed cases and the three well developed awns on the seed. The hummock grasses differ in their growth from the tufted or tussock grasses by their repeatedly branching stems, each branch terminating in a spiny leaf; these stems form roots where they touch the ground, growing in an outward and upward direction forming a distinct mound. In older plants the inner part of the plant may die and the continued outer growth forms a distinct ring, which may be up to 6 m in diameter. Spinifex does not grow on heavy clay soils, but is otherwise widespread. Individual plants are often more widely spaced than tufted grasses

but sometimes the hummocks may grow touching one another.

Triodia

One of the more widespread species is Lobed Spinifex, *Triodia basedowii,* which may be a compact to straggly tussock, 20 to 35 cm high and 75 cm wide, often forming rings 1 to 2 m across. The compact seed heads are carried on slender stalks. This species is common on sandplains and dunes. Another widespread smaller species is Porcupine Grass, *Triodia irritans,* which forms a compact tussock about 60 cm high and to about 1 m wide, and has fine prickly leaves; the seed heads are looser and more slender than in *T. basedowii.* This species grows chiefly on rocky slopes.

a Cane Grass *Zygochloa paradoxa*
b Lobed Spinifex *Triodia basedowii*
c Porcupine Grass *Triodia irritans*
d Gummy Spinifex *Triodia pungens*
e Feathertop Spinifex *Plectrachne schinzii*

Great Grey or Buck Spinifex, *T. longiceps,* with greyish green, stiff, prickly leaves, forms large tussocks up to 1 m high and 1.5 to 2 m in width, sometimes rings up to 6 m across.

Plectrachne

There are four species of *Plectrachne* in the area. One of the species, Feathertop Spinifex or Silvery Spinifex, *P. schinzii,* is widespread and common on the sand dunes north of the South Australian border. It forms dense tussocks 30 cm high and 90 cm in diameter with numerous seed heads to 1 m in height.

b

d

Fauna

Central Australia is rich in certain types of fauna which vary from the large Red Kangaroo to the many small nocturnal animals such as marsupial mice, numerous birds, reptiles, fish and still smaller life such as insects and spiders. In addition to the natural inhabitants, there are also introduced species which have escaped and established themselves as feral animals.

As the vegetation of the area grows rapidly with the availability of moisture, so the fauna varies in number with good and bad seasons.

Adaptation to the Environment

Over the millenia, the fauna of the area have adapted to the arid conditions and extremes in temperature to which they are subjected. In hot arid areas dehydration and overheating of the body are problems for the various forms of life.

Some amphibious creatures in the area such as frogs, fish and other small forms of water life, can bury themselves or their eggs in the mud of waterholes and, when the water has completely dried up, are able to live in a state of almost suspended animation for long periods with the mud acting as an insulator; some types of eggs can survive complete desiccation. When it eventually rains, the creatures and eggs become reactivated, grow rapidly and reproduce until the dry conditions come again, when the same cycle is repeated.

Many animals have evolved measures to reduce loss of body moisture: sweat glands may be absent, greatly reducing evaporation from the skin; urine is concentrated and minimal; faeces pass from the body in an almost dry state.

The surface coverings of the skin, such as fur and feathers, are important, as they serve as insulators for the body. These coverings can be loosened or tightened by the animal or bird to increase or decrease its insulating properties. In direct contrast to the above, reptiles have a covering of scales which have negligible insulating properties and, as they are cold blooded animals with no mechanism to control body temperatures, they are particularly vulnerable to temperature changes. They are dependent upon heat for their activity, but can only spend limited time in the full sun as they soon become over-heated. Similarly, during cold periods, they are completely inactive.

To protect themselves against extremes in temperature, animals, birds and other creatures make use of trees, grass and other plants, logs, bark, burrows, rocks, crevices in rocks and caves or other similar places to provide suitable protection, becoming active when conditions suit their requirements, usually during the early morning and late afternoon or evening. As a further measure, many small creatures confine themselves to nocturnal activity.

Feeding and Drinking

As water and moisture are necessities for all living creatures, most animals feed in the early morning whilst the dew is present, or in the late afternoon or evening when conditions are less extreme. The dew which forms on herbage and other objects is an important supplementary source of water for dwellers in arid areas and, for some creatures, is their only source of water.

The nature of its diet influences each creature's need for water; for example, those which live on nectar or eat insects and other forms of animal life can obtain all or most of their fluid needs by this means. Similarly, herbivorous animals obtain fluids from the vegetation they eat, which reduces their need to drink, and animals such as kangaroos can exist for a week, or even longer, without drinking.

In contrast to the above, grain eating birds such as budgerigars and Zebra Finches usually require water daily.

Breeding Habits

During extended periods of drought when sources of food are no longer available, some of the more mobile species, such as kangaroos and birds, are able to migrate to areas where conditions are more favourable. As a further measure, during dry periods breeding is greatly reduced or may even not take place, and so the number of animals, birds and other creatures in the area may be greatly reduced.

With the advent of rain and rapid growth of plants in the area, the fauna have the capacity to breed rapidly. Birds soon begin nesting, and quickly produce a clutch of eggs followed by hatchlings. Some types, such as budgerigars, may produce a second clutch of eggs before the young birds of the last clutch have left the nest. Similarly, insects, spiders and the like, rapidly increase in numbers as plants grow and, in turn, provide a source of food for predators.

The Impact of Man and Introduced Animals

As described above, the fauna of the area live in a delicate balance and even minor changes may have drastic effect upon them. The removal of dead plants, branches, logs and stones from the ground can result in loss of habitat for some small creatures.

The clearing of land and introduction of grazing animals such as cattle and horses can play havoc with the native flora. Grazing animals compete with the natural inhabitants for food and water, particularly during extended periods of drought. The hard hoofs of these heavy animals trample and destroy small burrows and holes in the ground which are the homes of small ground dwelling marsupials and rodents. Overgrazing brings about erosion and loss of many plants, with the subsequent loss of food and habitat for the fauna.

A number of animals introduced for different purposes, such as the fox, domestic cat, horse, donkey, camel and cow, have been abandoned or escaped into the area. These animals have established themselves and bred and now live as individuals or groups, sometimes large groups, in the area, where they compete with native animals for food and destroy their habitats. Foxes and, in particular, feral cats continue to kill large numbers of native fauna who have little defence against them.

a

b

Mammals

There are a number of mammals native to Central Australia, among them kangaroos, wallabies, dingoes, small marsupials and rodents, even the Spiny Anteater and a marsupial mole. Apart from kangaroos, euros, rock wallabies and an occasional dingo, the numerous small animals are rarely seen as they are nocturnal and remain in burrows, hollow logs, bark, under rocks, in caves or other places for protection during the day from the hot dry conditions to which they are subjected. Some of these animals sun themselves in the early morning when temperatures are lower. On sandy plains and sand dunes the tracks from the nightly activites of these small animals may be observed in the early mornings.

Animals commonly seen are discussed and the names of the small nocturnal creatures are mentioned.

The Kangaroo Family Macropodidae

There are many different species of the kangaroo family in Australia, with three occurring in the area.

Red Kangaroo *Macropus rufus*

The Red Kangaroo, the largest of all the kangaroos, with some males up to 2 m in height, occurs throughout the dry parts of Australia. These kangaroos are reddish to bluish grey above and a white colour underneath; there is a black and white patch around the nose and a broad white stripe on each side of the head from the mouth to the ear. The females, smaller than the males, are often bluish grey in colour. The Red Kangaroo occurs chiefly on flat grassy plains with trees and shrubs, such as mulga, which afford shade protection.

Euro, Common Wallaroo *Macropus robustus erubescens*

These animals are smaller than the Red Kangaroo and are reddish to dark grey above with a lighter colour beneath. The fur is short and shaggy in appearance and around the nostrils there is a distinct black area of skin. The male is usually larger and darker in colour than the female. This kangaroo stands with its shoulder well back and elbows tucked into the sides. Unlike the Red Kangaroo which keeps to the flat country, the Euro inhabits stony rises and rocky hills, feeding in adjoining grasses and shrubs, but sometimes extending to the edges of the plains around the hills to feed. Like the Red Kangaroo, the Euro can survive for periods without drinking.

Rock Wallaby *Petrogale*

As well as being smaller than other members of the kangaroo family, the rock wallaby differs in the following: the claw of the fourth toe of

a Red Kangaroo *Macropus rufus*
b A young grey Euro *Macropus robustus erubescens*
c Black-footed Rock Wallaby with a joey in its pouch *Petrogale lateralis*

the hindfoot projects only slightly beyond the large toe pad; the soles of the rear feet are rough and granulated with an obvious fringe of stiff hairs, both characteristics which enable the animal to climb rocks. The tail is less tapered than that of the kangaroo and is carried arched over the back when hopping. There are ten different rock wallabies in Australia, some having subspecies and races which are restricted to particular areas.

Black-footed Rock Wallaby *Petrogale lateralis*

There are three subspecies of this wallaby in Australia with two distinct races, including the one in the Macdonnell Ranges. These animals, about half a metre high, are reddish brown above and grey on the neck and shoulders, with a white stripe on the cheeks, a black and white stripe on the back, and a white stripe on the sides; the tail is brownish grey to black with a brush at the end. This rock wallaby lives amongst the rocky outcrops in the Macdonnell Ranges and is commonly seen in Simpson's Gap National Park. It feeds on grass and the leaves of plants which grow between the rocks. As with the kangaroos, they seem to be able to survive for periods without drinking. During the day they rest in shaded crevices and caves, emerging to feed chiefly in the early morning, late afternoon or evening.

Small Mammals

Throughout the area there are a number of small animals which live in burrows and protected positions during the day, emerging at night to feed. Some may sun themselves for periods in the early morning when temperatures are less extreme. With the clearing of areas and introduction of grazing, there has been a change in the habitats of these small animals. In addition, with feral cats and foxes destroying many, some of the small creatures are becoming rare and a few are now endangered species.

Carnivorous Marsupials

These are small mouse-like creatures. Mulgara, Crested-tailed Marsupial-mouse, *Dasycercus cristicauda;* Fat-Tailed Marsupial Mouse, Fat-tailed Antechinus, *Pseudantechinus macdonnellensis;* Ooldea Dunnart, *Sminthopsis ooldea;* Fat-tailed Dunnart, *Sminthopsis crassicaudata;* Hairy-footed Dunnart, Hairy-footed Pouched Mouse, *Sminthopsis hirtipes;* Wongai Ningaui, Stripe-faced Dunnart, *Sminthopsis macroura;* Kultarr, *Antechinomys laniger.*

Marsupial Mole *Notoryctes typhlops*

This is Australia's only mole and spends most of its life underground in the desert sands. It is blind and is a beautiful golden sandy colour.

Bandicoots

There is only one bandicoot in the area, the rare Bilby or Rabbit-eared Bandicoot, *Macrotis lagotis.* The other species are believed to be extinct.

Possum

There is one possum in the area, the Common Brushtail Possum, *Trichosurus vulpecula.*

Rodents

There are a number of native rats and mice in Australia, with several of them occurring in the area.

Rats Water Rat, *Hydromys chrysogaster;* Plains Rat, *Pseudomys australis;* Central Rock-rat, *Zyzomys pedunculatus;* Long Haired Rat, *Rattus villosissimus.*

Mice Desert Mouse, *Pseudomys desertor;* Sandy Inland Mouse, *Pseudomys hermannsburgensis;* Spinifex Hopping-mouse, *Notomys alexis;* Fawn Hopping-mouse, *Notomys cervinus;* Forrest's Mouse, *Leggadina forrestii;* Introduced House Mouse, *Mus musculus.*

Spiny Anteater, Short Beaked Echidna *Tachyglossus aculeatus*

The one Australian species is distributed throughout the continent but, as it is mainly

Top: Spiny Anteater *Tachyglossus aculeatus*
Above: Dingo *Canis familiaris dingo*

nocturnal in its activities, is rarely seen. This animal, which lives on ants, has the head extended into a beak and the furry body covered with spines. When disturbed, it rolls up into a ball or digs itself rapidly and vertically into the ground, leaving its spines exposed.

Dingo *Canis familiaris dingo*

Some authorities believe that the dingo, which is one of a group of primitive dogs, is a newer member of the Australian fauna, having come to the continent with the early Aborigines. It is commonly ginger to sandy in colour with white feet, but some are black. Dingo tracks are often seen, and the animal itself may be seen in ones and twos in the early morning, particularly in reserve areas of the Macdonnell Ranges, and sometimes will not hesitate to come quite close to people. They are predators of various mammals, birds and reptiles, but will eat almost anything when food is scarce.

Bats

There are about fourteen different types of native bat in the area. They congregate in rock crevices and caves, holes in trees and other places which provide protection during the day. They are small animals with a body length of about 50 to 75 mm and feed on moths, beetles, mosquitoes and other insects.

Feral Mammals

As previously discussed, there are a number of introduced animals which have become feral or wild throughout the area and occur in varying numbers.

Feral Cat *Felis catus*

Descendants of the domestic cat are established as feral animals throughout Australia. These wild cats are larger and more vicious than the domestic variety, and live in logs, under shrubs, in burrows and other places which make them difficult to detect. They are active in the evening and at night, when they destroy large numbers of fauna of different types who have little or no protection against them.

Fox *Vulpes vulpes*

This animal was originally introduced into Australia for sporting purposes and has spread throughout the continent, only excepting the far northern tropical areas. This reddish brown animal with white below is a serious pest, as it kills large numbers of native fauna which have no protection against it. Like the dingo, the fox is active in the evening and early morning and is sometimes seen slinking away into vegetation.

Donkey *Equus asinus*

Donkeys were originally introduced to Australia in the early days of settlement as working animals, but when they were no longer needed they were often abandoned. As these animals originally came from dry regions, they have established themselves in the arid parts of Australia, where they occur in pairs or with a number in a group; they are commonly seen in remote areas. These grazing animals compete with the native species for food and water, and with their hard hoofs destroy burrows and other protective habitats of small animals. With other grazing animals, they may denude a whole area. When in groups they may take possession of a waterhole and deny access to other animals.

Horse *Equus caballus*

Over the years many domestic horses have escaped or been abandoned and established themselves as feral animals, commonly known

as brumbies. These horses live in small to large herds and do similar damage to donkeys.

Camel *Camelus dromedarius*

The one-humped camel was introduced in the early days of exploration in Australia. For many years they were used for exploration and transporting goods in inland Australia, but with the decline in their use, animals were released and escaped into the surrounding areas. As they are particularly adapted to arid conditions, they have become feral animals in the central and western desert areas of Australia. These large, gingery to sandy coloured animals, with a distinct hump, occur in small and large herds. They constitute further competition for native grazing animals and interfere with the ground habitats of small animals.

Left: Donkeys *Equus asinus*
Above: Camel *Camelus dromedarius*

Rabbit *Oryctolgus cuniculus*

The rabbit, which was introduced into Australia in the mid eighteen hundreds, has spread across the continent and is well established in the area, even in such places as the middle of the Simpson Desert. This animal is most destructive to plants, for, as well as eating green herbage, they dig up and eat the roots. During dry periods they even eat the bark of trees and shrubs, often resulting in their loss. As well as competing with the native fauna for food and damaging vegetation, their activities lead to soil erosion.

Birds

There are many beautiful birds in the area with over 200 different kinds having been recorded. The numbers vary with the season, availability of food and water and the time of the year. Some types of birds may remain in particular areas for an extended period, e.g. the Pied Butcher Bird and Spinifex Pigeon, whilst others, such as the Rainbow or Bee Bird, remain for a while and then move on.

The birds vary in size from the small Zebra Finch and dainty wrens to the large bustard, brolga and emu. They also differ in their habits. Some may occur singly or occasionally in pairs, like the Willie Wagtail; the gregarious types, such as the Zebra Finch, budgerigars, galah and corella, may occur in large flocks, especially when moving from one area to another and to sources of drinking water, and, in particular, when roosting in the evening in trees around waterholes.

As many birds, particularly the seed eaters, require water daily, the greatest number of different types occurs in the vicinity of permanent waterholes with adjoining trees and shrubs to give them protection against predators such as hawks and falcons.

Larger birds, such as the bustard and emu prefer open places and wooded areas, whilst the brolga confines itself chiefly to moist vegetated plains.

The handsome Wedgetail Eagle and other birds of prey, such as falcons, kites and hawks, prefer the lightly vegetated areas, in order to observe their prey more readily.

Numbers of water birds are controlled by the availability of large, long lasting areas of water which provide them with food, mainly various forms of aquatic life and water plants. During dry periods, the number of birds is greatly reduced, with birds such as ducks and pelicans migrating out of drought stricken areas to others more favourable. Cormorants and such like move from one permanent water hole to another along the larger watercourses.

Whilst many different types of birds are observed in the area at different times, the following are some of the birds more frequently seen.

Smaller Birds

Pied Butcher Bird *Cracticus nigrogularis*

This handsome black and white magpie-like bird makes its presence known in the early

Left: Pied Butcher Bird *Cracticus nigrogularis*
Above: Spinifex Pigeon *Petrophassa plumifera*

morning and evening by its lyrical extended song.

Spinifex Pigeon *Petrophassa plumifera*

This brown pigeon, with attractive markings and a tufted crest, has distinctive markings around the eyes. It is common in areas of the Macdonell Ranges and spends most of its time on the ground feeding on grass seed. Its call is a gentle typical pigeon 'coo'.

Crested Pigeon *Ocyphaps lophotes*

This beautiful pigeon, with bluish grey tonings and bronze marked wings, feeds on grass seed and frequents areas adjoining waterways.

Zebra Finch *Poephila guttata*

These gregarious, seed-eating finches are the commonest of the small birds in the area and frequent grasslands in the vicinity of permanent water with adjoining trees and shrubs, commonly in large flocks. They have a grey head, zebra-like breast and brown wings, with white on brown spotted side markings. They make a rather monotonous continuous cheep.

Painted Finch, Painted Firetail *Emblema picta*

This beautiful small finch inhabits spinifex country particularly around rocky hills and gorges where there are permanent water holes. Unlike the Zebra Finch, they occur mainly in pairs and small groups. The face, neck, breast and back of tail are red, the wings and top of head brown, and the sides of the body black with white spots.

Little Corella *Cacatua sanguinea*

This white cockatoo with reddish-pink colour on the head and a blue section around the eyes, is common in areas where there is permanent water. These birds, which feed on the seed of grasses and other plants in the early morning and afternoon, are often seen in pairs and small groups during the day resting in trees, but at roosting time they congregate in large number in trees adjoining permanent water holes along watercourses, where they set up an incessant shrieking din which may continue in bursts during the night. They are destructive birds, biting off branches of trees in which they rest, and, in areas where they congregate, the trees may be killed.

Pink Cockatoo, Major Mitchell's Cockatoo *Cacatua leadbeateri*

This beautiful bird with reddish-pink tonings, particularly under the wings, has a crest which, when extended, has a distinctive band of red and yellow markings. This parrot spends much time on the ground feeding on the seeds and roots of various plants, then flying off with a shriek to the nearest tree when disturbed; it occurs in pairs and groups.

Red Tailed Cockatoo *Calyptorhynchus magnificus*

These large handsome black cockatoos with black plumage have bright red feathers in the tail which show to advantage as the bird is flying; the female is duller in colour and has yellow spots on the head and neck. These birds are tree dwelling types, feeding on seeds of such trees as Desert Oak and eucalypt. They also dig out and eat grubs from the bark of trees. They usually occur in pairs or small groups.

Budgerigars *Melopsittacus undulatus*

These small members of the parrot family are widely distributed and occur in large flocks. In the wild budgerigars are green with yellow, black and blue markings, in contrast to the domesticated birds which come in a range of blues, greens, yellows and whites, which are the result of intensive selection and breeding of desired types. These birds feed on grass seed, favouring various types at different times of the year. They occur on grassy plains, but within flying distance of a source of water. In good seasons these birds breed rapidly and flocks may vary from a few hundred to several thousand.

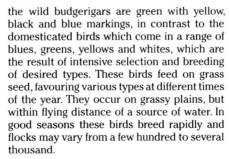

a   Crested Pigeon *Ocyphaps lophotes*
b   Zebra Finch *Peophila guttata*
c   Pink Cockatoo *Cacatua leadbeateri*
d   Red-tailed Black Cockatoo *Calyptorhynchus magnificus*
e   Budgerigars *Melopsittacus undulatus*
f   Galah *Cacatua roseicapilla*

Galah *Cacatua roseicapilla*

This widespread cockatoo, with an attractive pink neck and breast and soft grey wings and head, occurs in pairs or small to large flocks and feeds on the seeds of grass and other plants, as well as the fleshy roots of some plants. These birds, when disturbed on the ground, fly off, and, when in a flock, present a delightful sight of pink and grey.

Cockateel
Leptolophus hollandicus

These small attractive parrots, with brown and white wings and yellow and red markings on the head, have a slender tufted crest. They are commonly in pairs or small to large groups, often along watercourses and waterholes with a covering of grass, shrubs and trees, feeding on the seed of grass and other plants.

Port Lincoln Ringed Neck Parrot *Barnardius zonarius*

This small parrot in colours of green, blue and yellow, has a distinctive yellow ring around the top of the neck. It occurs in pairs or small groups in areas of trees, shrubs and grass, adjoining sources of water, feeding on grass seed and blossom.

Rainbow Bird, Bee Eater
Merops ornatus

This beautiful bird with an extended tail is strikingly marked in green, blue, brown, yellow and white with distinctive markings around the eyes. It occurs in various areas, resting on dead branches of trees, stumps or other similar positions, from where it makes short rapid flights to catch its diet of bees, flies and other insects. The Rainbow Bird is migratory, spending a period in the area, then moving to other parts.

Mistletoe Bird
Dicaeum hirundinaceum

These small birds commonly occur in pairs, with the male dark blue on the back and wings and scarlet on the breast and the female brownish in colour. They frequent trees and shrubs on which mistletoe grows, feeding on the mistletoe fruits, and are responsible for the spread of these parasitic plants.

Fairy Martin
Hylochelidon ariel

These dainty swallows with a reddish brown head, white breast, bluish back and brown wings, are found in small to large groups around watercourses and waterholes. They remain in an area for extended periods while there is a plentiful supply of the insects which they catch on the wing, and migrate to other areas when their source of food is no longer available. They build bottleshaped mud nests which they attach to suitable supports protected from the weather, such as under a bridge, or in crevices in rocky walls.

Large Birds
Bustard, Plain Turkey
Ardeotis australis

This large turkey-like bird with a rather stiff appearance has brown wings, and a white flat head with black top and white neck. It occurs in plains areas with shrubs and trees, standing like a sentinel before moving off. It feeds on the foliage and seed of plants, and on insects. Once plentiful, these large birds now occur only as individuals or pairs in outlying areas.

Brolga *Grus rubicundus*

Sometimes known as the Native Companion, this member of the crane family is a large bird with a soft plumage of a delicate shade of grey; the head is marked with red. These large birds, commonly occurring in pairs or groups, are inhabitants of low-lying moist plain areas. They feed on various types of small creatures such as frogs, worms and insects, also various types of plants, particularly those with fleshy roots which they easily remove from the ground with their strong beaks. They make a trumpeting sound and perform delightful dances in which they move their wings in a rhythmic manner.

Emu
Dromaius novaehollandiae

The emu is Australia's largest bird with its head sometimes as much as 2 m above the ground. It has long powerful legs and three spreading toes. The feathers, which are light brown to almost black in old birds, are rather plumose and hang loosely over the body, forming an excellent insulator against both hot and cold conditions; thus, these birds are able to spend considerable time in the open during the heat of the day. They occur in various types of country and eat a variety of food including the leaves, flowers, seeds and fruit of plants such as *Eremophila* and quandong, and insects and other small creatures.

Wedge Tail Eagle
Aquila audax

This large, rather majestic eagle with a wingspan of over 2 m, has a distinct wedge-shaped tail and brown plumage. It ranges over a wide area and is sometimes seen hovering in the sky or resting on the limb of a dead tree, rock ledge or other position which gives a good view of the surrounding area. They prey on various animals and large birds.

Black Kite, Forked-tailed Kite *Milvus migrans*

This bird with dark brown plumage and a forked tail is common around settlements, where a group is often observed hovering. They prey on various small animals and are efficient scavengers.

Grey Falcon
Falco hypoleucus

This bird of prey is one of several falcons in the area, which plunge down at a rapid rate to catch their prey while still on the wing. The

a   Two Bustards blend in with the surrounding vegetation *Ardeotis australis*
b   Brolga *Grus rubicundus*
c   Emu *Dromaius novaehollandiea*
d   Grey Falcon *Falco hypoleucus*
e   Two Wedge Tail Eagles come to feed on a euro killed by a car

feathers on the wings, tail and head are mid-grey with a lighter colour around the neck and breast. The Grey Falcon shown on page 72 had been preying on a group of Zebra Finches, some of which, shown on page 71, escaped by flying into the protection offered by the sharply pointed foliage of the Dead Finish Wattle, *Acacia tetragonophylla.*

Water Birds

Where there are large bodies of water for extended periods in the area, water birds of different types are seen. Amongst these are the pelican, *Pelicanus conspicillatus,* cormorants,

ducks of different types, egrets, herons and Black Swans. As the water dries up, so the number of water birds in the area decreases.

Wood Duck, Maned Duck or Goose *Chenonetta jubata*

The female bird shown here with its young ducklings is one of a number of ducks which inhabit the area when conditions are suitable. The male Maned Duck has darker markings on the head and tail than the female; the wings are light grey while the female's are mottled. These birds inhabit watercourses with well-wooded margins. Unlike most ducks, they perch in trees.

Wood Duck *Chenonetta jubata*

Reptiles

The reptiles are a group of vertebrate animals differing from mammals in that they are cold blooded and have no mechanism to control their body temperature; the skin has a layer of scales which may be thin or horny. Reptiles are dependent upon warmth for their activity and during cold periods may become completely inactive, furthermore they can only spend a limited time in the sun before their bodies become overheated. Within the area there are a few snakes, and a number of different lizards belonging to several families.

Geckoes

The geckoes belong to the family Gekkonidae in which there are about eight different genera. These small nocturnal lizards generally have soft bodies, usually with thin skin and non-overlapping scales, although some species having projecting spines; the eyes, which are without lids, project and the lizard cleans them with its tongue; the toes of some types have sticky pads, whilst others have claws; the tail tends to unusual shapes, varying from broad and flattened to round and thick. Some species use the tail to store fat, on which they exist during cold periods and when food is unavailable. These small creatures live under bark, in cracks in logs, under rocks and crevices, in holes in the ground or in other situations which protect them from the sun, cold and predators. Their diet consists of insects, spiders or even small lizards. A number of the species appear to be similar. An example of the group is shown.

Beaked Gecko *Rhychoedura ornata* A small soft lizard with protruding eyes, a dark brown pattern along the back and cream spots along the sides, and a swollen tail.

Skinks

The skinks, the largest group of lizards in Australia, belong to the family Scincidae, with about nine different genera. They are probably better known than other lizards, as the small Grass Skink, *Lampropholis guichenoti,* is common around houses and gardens. The skinks, with a few exceptions, are smooth with shiny scales; the head is tapered and snake-like and the tail is mostly long and slender. Many skinks can shed their tails to elude a predator and can then grow another one.

One of the largest of the skinks is the Blue Tongue Lizard, *Tiliqua scincoides,* common around Australia. Its close relative is the Central Australian species *Tiliqua multifasciata,* which is a stout lizard with blackish brown and yellowish orange bands across the body. Some skinks are legless or almost so and resemble small snakes, but differ in having ear openings. Skinks live under various objects which will provide shelter, or they may burrow into loose soil. Their diet consists of insects or other small creatures.

Shingle-back Lizard *Tiliqua rugosa* This stout bodied lizard with a short stumpy tail has distinct raised pinecone-like scales and varies in colour from brownish yellow to black. When surprised, it opens its blue mouth, bends its body and hisses. It occurs in grassland and woodland areas.

Left: Beaked Gecko *Rhynchoedura ornata*
Above: Bearded Dragon *Togona viticeps*

Dragons

The dragons belong to the family Agamidae with about seven different genera. These lizards are distinguished from geckoes and skinks by their thick rough scales, usually with spiny projections, their lidded eyes, and their tails which cannot regenerate when broken off. The dragons can present a rather fearsome apearance; when surprised, they open their brightly orange or yellow coloured mouth, make a hissing noise and raise themselves, lifting their spine. But in direct contrast, they sometimes remain completely motionless. These lizards may bite, but do not have poisonous fangs. Unlike most lizards, their tough skin enables them to withstand hot arid conditions. They can run at a rapid rate, sometimes on their hind legs. These lizards live in holes in the ground, under clumps of spinifex, logs, rocks and similar positions. Their diet consists of insects, spiders, mice and other small creatures.

Bearded Dragon *Togona viticeps* This lizard in colours of grey, yellow and black, has a wide body and a long tapered tail. The skin is rough and scaly with rows of spines around the neck, the sides of the body, and on the legs and tail.

Above: Thorny Devil *Moloch horridus*
Right: Perenti *Varanus giganteus*

Thorny Devil *Moloch horridus* This rather grotesque lizard is brownish in colour with distinct yellow, cream and white markings. There are rather awesome projecting spines over the body, but these are soft and merely a device to deter predators. The diet consists chiefly of black ants.

Frilled Dragon *Chlamydosaurus kingii* This lizard with a broad body and long tapered tail has a folded frill around the neck which it can raise into a wide collar, at the same time opening its mouth, to present an awesome appearance when surprised.

Long Nosed Dragon *Gemmataphora longirostris* This long greyish dragon with lighter markings is frequently seen along watercourses in the Macdonnell Ranges.

Goannas

The goannas or monitors, Australia's largest lizards, belong to the family Varanidae which has one genus. They have a tough, leathery scaly skin, a long neck, tapered head and a long powerful tail which does not grow again if broken off. They have strong legs and the toes have sharp claws. These lizards are grey to blackish in colour with yellow markings. They are able to run rapidly and climb trees very fast. They live in hollow logs and trees, burrows, holes in the ground and under large rocks. Diet is wide and includes various forms of insects and animals, whether dead or alive. The largest of the species is discussed.

Perentie *Varanus giganteus* This large lizard grows to 2 m or more in length. It is brownish on the back and sides, with rows of yellow spots on the back and tail; it is yellowish beneath the body.

Snakes

There are several different snakes in the area, including small non-venomous pythons to about 2 m long, such as the Children's Python, *Liasis childreni.* The widespread King Brown Snake, *Pseudechis australis,* occurs in the area. This snake is a venomous species and grows to about 2 m long. Although snakes inhabit the area, they are rarely seen.

Arthropods

Within the area there are numerous small creatures belonging to a group known as Arthropoda, which have jointed segments of the body and legs, with an outer shell to support the body in lieu of an internal skeleton. In this group are included the insects, arachnids, crustaceans and myriopods.

Insects

Insects have a head, thorax, abdomen, six legs and often wings and include ants, beetles, moths, flies, mosquitoes and the like. Although insects do considerable damage to plant life, they are a source of food for animals, birds and reptiles. Although insects such as flies are active during the day, most are active at night and shelter in various protected positions during the day. Evidence of their nightly activity is often observed as tracks left on sandplains and dunes in the early morning.

Ants

Amongst the many different ants, the Mulga Ant, *Polyrachis macropus,* is of interest. It is a black nocturnal species, which prefers the vicinity of mulgas and builds a crater-like nest above the ground surface, formed of soil and covered with dead mulga leaves. Another unusual ant is the Honey-pot Ant, *Camponotus inflatus,* which is closely related to the common sugar ant, *Camponotus nigriceps.* The Honey-pot ant feeds on the sweet sap obtained from lerps and scale insects. The surplus sugary sap is carried back to the nest and continually fed to newly hatched ants until the abdomen becomes so distended that they are unable to move. This stored honey is then

Mulga Ants Nest *Polyrachis macropus*

regurgitated to worker ants as required. These ants are dug up from the ground by Aborigines and the honey is sucked from the abdomen.

Jumper Ants Another group of ants which make their presence felt by their bite is the Jumper Ant, a common species of which *Myrmecia nigrocincta,* a yellow and black ant, has a jumping movement which can create a stir when their nest is unnoticed.

Moths

Amongst the innumerable different species of moths are the large Wood or Goat Moths, *Xyleutes.* These large nocturnal moths may have a thick abdomen and wide wingspan. The larvae live in the trunks of trees such as the acacia where they remain for several years before pupating and emerging as a moth. The Witchetty Grub, *Xyleutes leucomochla,* favours *Acacia kempiana* and attacks the base of the trunk and roots at or below ground level. The large white larvae are regarded as a delicacy by Aborigines.

Flies

Amongst the many flies, the Bush Fly, *Musca vetustissima,* is the most annoying of all insects. This fly breeds in decaying vegetation and animal droppings. The problem is greatly accentuated by the droppings from larger animals such as cattle and horses. Efforts have been made to introduce a dung beetle which collects pieces of animal droppings to bury as food for its young.

Dragon and Damsel Flies This interesting group of double winged insects includes the large dragon flies and smaller damsel flies, belonging to the Odonata group. These insects feed on mosquitoes and other insects which they catch and eat whilst in flight. Both types spend their developing life or nymphal stage as aquatic insects. The larva of the dragon fly has a voracious appetite for all types of small aquatic life such as mosquitoes, tadpoles and even small fish.

Beetles

This large group of insects belongs to the order Coleoptera, in which there are innumerable types of beetles from small to large and from dull coloured browns to brightly coloured and shiny black types. Most are nocturnal species and can produce many interesting patterns in the sand during the night. Some of the species are carnivorous and eat insects and other small creatures.

Bugs

There are many different types of bugs all of which belong to the order Hemiptera and have a sucking beak. There are some types which attack other insects, such as the Assassin or Reduviid Bugs, which catch and kill other insects by sucking the juices from their bodies. Others such as the Water Scorpions, Water Bugs and Water Boatmen, which live an aquatic life, catch and kill various types of aquatic animals.

Various types of bugs attack plants with some species being favoured more than others. The hibiscus family is a favourite host to a number of different species and *Hibiscus* and *Gossypium* are often found with numerous bugs on the flowers.

Bag Moths

The hairy larvae of the Bag Moth, called Processionary Caterpillars, *Terara contraria,* construct a bag of web in the branches of trees, such as mulga, in which they shelter during the day. At night these caterpillars come out in a procession and feed on the leaves of the tree or adjoining trees where their web bag is located. The hairs of these caterpillars can cause intense irritation when they come in contact with a person's skin. As the bag contains the cast off skins of the larvae and their excreta, they should be avoided at all costs; contact with the bag may bring about intense irritation, particularly if the dust gets into the eyes.

Mosquitoes

There are several different species of mosquitoes in the area, the intensity of their

numbers varying with the presence of areas of water in which to breed.

Grasshoppers

There are many different types and colours of grasshoppers in the area. These grasshoppers have short horns and belong mainly to the family Acrididae, to which the plague hoppers belong.

Termites

Termites belong to a group of insects known as Isoptera and are commonly called white ants, but they differ from the true ants which belong to a family known as Formicidae, part of the order Hymenoptera, to which the bees and wasps belong. There are a number of different types of termites which live in close social

Top: Bag Moths' Nest *Terara contraria*
Above: Termites Nest *Coptotermes*

communities and build galleried nests from clay, below or above the ground. Termites eat wood and other forms of cellulose, such as grass. They make underground galleries from their nest to the source of food and can do considerable damage to timber. Some types harvest grass which they store in their nest. Some termites build mounds above the ground; in the northern part of the area nests may be several metres high. The Magnetic Termite, *Amitermes meridionalis,* of northern Australia, builds large mounds more or less in a north-south direction. Some members of the Coptotermes build rounded mounds above the ground, whilst such species as *Masutitermes triodiae* build very tall nests.

Arachnids

This group of arthropods belong to an order known as Arachnida and includes the spiders, scorpions, ticks and mites. They have an abdomen, but differ from insects in having the head and thorax fused together and having eight legs.

Spiders

There are a number of different types of spiders in the area, including ground dwellers and those which inhabit the branches of trees and shrubs and other plants.

Wolf Spiders These spiders, belonging to the family Lycosidae, construct a hole in the ground which they often line with web. They frequently form a lip of leaves and web or cover the hole with a lid. They are greyish to greyish yellow or light brown, often with a pattern on the back and have long legs.

Huntsmen Spiders These spiders belong to the family Sporossidae, with some commonly known as tarantulas. They are usually large and hairy, brown to brownish grey in colour, with long legs and a flattened body. They live under loose bark on trees and similar positions.

Orb Weavers This large group of spiders belong to two families, Argiopidae and Epedridae. They are often large, with a soft swollen abdomen, finely hairy legs and coloured markings on the body. They spin circular webs between the branches of plants in order to trap passing insects.

Scorpions

The scorpions belong to the Scorpionidae group, which is also included in the larger group Arachnida, to which spiders also belong. As with spiders, they have eight legs, but in addition they have a pair of claws on jointed arms, somewhat like a crab, with which they catch insects and other small creatures which they eat. The abdomen is extended into a jointed tail with a curved sting at the end. When prey is caught, the tail is bent forward over the body and the sting is used to inject venom into the captive. Scorpions can inflict a

Golden Orb-Weaving Spider *Nephila maculata*

sting which is painful but not fatal, but this rarely occurs.

Two of the more common scorpions are *Lychas marmoreus,* a small species with a finely spotted pattern of greenish brown and grey, and a larger, widely distributed species, which extends into New Guinea, *Homorus caudicula,* which has a bulky body and slender short tail. Scorpions live under rocks, logs of wood and the like.

When camping in areas where scorpions occur in numbers, it is not uncommon to find one or more under a ground sheet.

Myriopods

This group, Diplopoda, belongs to the spider group and has numerous body segments with a pair of legs to each segment. it includes different types of centipedes and millipedes, the latter being quite harmless creatures.

Centipedes There are a number of different types of centipedes which have their first pair of legs modified into poison glands, which they use to sting insects and other small creatures before eating them. They are chiefly nocturnal and live under rocks and in holes in the ground. They can give a nasty sting, but this rarely occurs.

Aquatic Life

In addition to the various water bugs and beetles found in ponds and watercourses, there are also different types of fish, shrimps and frogs.

Fish

There are some 30 different types of fish in the area, most of which are small, although some may grow up to 30 cm in length. The fish occur in permanent waterholes, watercourses and gullies. Some of the species are able to bury themselves and their eggs in the mud at the bottom of a waterhole and, when the water dries up, may remain in a state of almost suspended animation for extended periods, becoming active once more when the pools fill with water.

Amongst the fish which are sometimes seen in the clearer pools in the Macdonnell Ranges is a spotted fish known as the Spangled Perch, Rainbow Fish or Striped Grunter.

Frogs

There are several different types of frog in the area which have adapted to the arid conditions. One such is the Water-holding Frog, which is able to fill its body with water and bury itself and its eggs in mud in the bottom of water-holes and in the sand when the waterhole dries up, remaining buried for an extended period, until rain causes it to resume its normal activity.

Crustacea

These animals with an outer shell belong to the same group as lobsters and crabs and are represented in the area. In the permanent waterholes of the larger rivers, such as the Diamantina, there are crayfish which resemble small lobsters, some species having only one developed claw. Of particular interest are the small unusual shrimps sometimes seen in small pools, such as the Shield Shrimp, *Triops australiens* and the Shelled Fairy Shrimp, *Limnadopsis birchii*. The eggs of these shrimps can become desiccated when a pool of water dries up and remain in this condition for extended periods, rapidly developing into adults when rains come.

Sunrise on the eastern edge of the Gibson Desert

Sunset on Coopers Creek in flood

Bibliography

BLACK J.M. *Flora of South Australia* Parts II, III, IV, Government Printer, Adelaide, 1964, 1963, 1957.

BLOMBERY A.M. *Australian Native Plants* Angus and Robertson, Sydney, 1980.

BLOMBERY A.M. *What Wildflower is That?* Lansdowne Press, Sydney, 1984.

CUNNINGHAM C.M., MULHAM W.E., MILTHORPE P.L., LEIGH J.H. *The Plants of Western New South Wales* Government Printer, Sydney, 1981.

DAVEY K. *Australian Desert Life* Landsdowne Press, Melbourne, 1969.

DAVEY K. *Australian Lizards* Lansdowne Press, Sydney, 1970.

HILL R. *Australian Birds* Nelson, Sydney, 1967.

IMMELMAN K. *Australian Finches* Angus and Robertson, Sydney, 1965.

JENNINGS J.N., MABBUTT J.A., (ed.) *Landform Studies from Australia and New Guinea* Australian National University Press, Canberra, 1967.

JESSUP J. (ed.) *Flora of Central Australia* A.H. and A.W. Reed (for Australian Systematic Botany Society) Sydney, 1981.

LASERON C.F. *The Face of Australia* Angus and Robertson, 1975.

LAZARIDES M. *The Grasses of Central Australia* Australian National University Press, Canberra, 1970.

McMICHAEL D.F. (ed.) *A Treasury of Australian Wildlife* Ure Smith, Sydney, 1967.

RUTGERS A., GOULD J. *Birds of Australia* Methuen and Co., Great Britain, 1967.

SCOBLE J. *The Complete Book of Budgerigars* Landsdowne Press, Sydney, 1981.

SEVENTY V. & C. *Australian Birds* Rigby Publishers Ltd, Sydney, 1981.

STRAHAN R. (ed.) *The Australian Museum Complete Book of Australian Mammals* Angus and Robertson, Sydney, 1983.

WHEELER D.J.B., JACOBS S.W.L., NORTON B.L. *Grasses of New South Wales* University of New England Publishing Unit, Armidale, 1982.

Index

Page numbers *in italic* show the main text for an item. Page numbers **in bold** are for plates.